HANSELS AND GRETELS

Studies of Children in Institutions for the Mentally Retarded

Dorothea D. Braginsky
FAIRFIELD UNIVERSITY

Benjamin M. Braginsky
WESLEYAN UNIVERSITY

Holt, Rinehart and Winston, Inc.
NEW YORK   CHICAGO   SAN FRANCISCO   ATLANTA
DALLAS   MONTREAL   TORONTO   LONDON   SYDNEY

This book is dedicated to the "surplus" children

Foreword

The content of this book has helped me make sense of a number of observations that I made nearly three decades ago. As a psychologist in a large state school and colony, I worked closely with a group of fifty high-school age inmates, classified as "high-grade mental defectives." I prepared myself through library research and clinical conferences to look for moronic behavior. Naturally, I was perplexed when I could not differentiate the day-to-day social behavior of these inmates from "normal" adolescents. They could laugh at jokes, invent entertainment for their peers, discriminate between the "good guys" and the "bad guys," earn and spend money, engage in athletic contests, read and play music, and so on. To try to resolve the dissonance, I reviewed the case records of these boys and girls and discovered that they had "tested" as "feebleminded" or "borderline" at the time they had been referred to a local court for commitment (although some had "tested" higher at earlier times). The Stanford–Binet IQ's of this particular group ranged from a low of 65 to a high of 85. More important, the case records indicated that the referrals to the court were made primarily not on the basis of IQ but rather on the basis of the fact that these children were somehow regarded as surplus human material. No one wanted these children. To be sure, like their non-inmate peers, some had had a history of petty theft, truancy, and "lewd and lascivious conduct." Most had a record of "reading disability" and other school problems.

Thus the perplexing question: Why were these relatively complete children called "retarded" and warehoused in a state institution? One possible response to the question was that these children apparently reached a crossroads where a teacher, a social worker, a juvenile court worker, or other professional entertained the hypothesis of "feeblemindedness." If confirmed by a standard intelligence test, then a label such as "feebleminded," "retarded," or "moron" was applied. In keeping with the ethos that such persons needed help, they were sent to training schools which were designed presumably to make morons less moronic, or to train retardates to live with their "mental" deficits.

My research interests turned to other topics and the perplexing questions regarding "mental retardation" were left unresolved.

Now Dorothea and Ben Braginsky have answered the questions. They offer experiment and argument to demonstrate that so-called retardates are in fact undifferentiated from their unlabeled peers, committing themselves well on psychological dimensions relevant for adaptation in an imperfect and changing world. The "retardates," not unlike their extramural peers, display power strategies, adaptive styles, and the ability to take into account the roles of others in their own behavioral choices. In short, they are not psychologically different from other specimens of humanity. That these inmates are differentiated on sociopolitical dimensions as the result of identifiable familial, educational, legal, and bureaucratic occurrences is well documented.

The conclusions inferred from the data are more convincing than the time-worn notions that relate commitment residence in a training school to disordered brains, traumatized psyches, or unhappy combinations of genes. In tune with other recent analyses, the Drs. Braginsky depart from the empty and misleading doctrine that people who are declared surplus, undesirable, disreputable, unwanted, and the like have some fundamental deficit. Few have presented such clear-cut evidence to challenge the entrenched belief that "mental retardates" are flat-faced, humorless, vegetative, and immoral automata.

The employment of the conceptual and operational tools of modern behavioral science is refreshing. Goffman's concept of impression management, Jones' concept of ingratiation, Christie's concept of Machiavellianism, and other sophisticated notions are central constructs in a program of sociopsychological experimentation. The reader cannot help but be impressed by the ingenuity of the experiments and the clarity with which the authors describe their findings. Further, they inform the reader how such a linguistic development has subtly influenced social policy. The serious reader will appreciate the inclusion of the straightforward methodology. How, for example, does an investigator go about the task of inquiring into the subtle power plays of supposedly stupid, apolitical retardates? The appendix makes available to the reader the instruments employed and the painstaking efforts to look into the day-to-day adaptations of these unfortunate children—a far cry from the study of "feeblemindedness" via standard tests of abstract intelligence.

Philosophy of science articulations give this book a special coloring. The authors take pains to direct the reader to the process of reification and demonstrate how earlier euphemistic metaphors of deficit and defect have acquired an unwarranted ontological status that has influenced both theory and practice.

Theodore R. Sarbin
University of California
Santa Cruz

Preface

In our earlier work with mental patients we found that mental institutions function primarily as catchment areas which facilitate the "social sanitation" process of society. The concept of mental illness, when applied to the inmates of these institutions, was devoid of meaning, obfuscating and distorting completely the behavior of the patients. The reason for their incarceration was that they either could not or did not want to function in the mainstream of society. They were marginal members of the community —surplus people. Thus, mental hospitals as well as the mental health professionals help to keep society's "house in order" by removing from the mainstream its human debris.

Most of the inmates in mental institutions, however, are adults. Our hunch and our concern was that similar social sanitation problems exist with respect to children, particularly children who come from the marginal, surplus population. The only large-scale facilities available for the collection of discarded, unneeded children are the institutions for the mentally retarded. We turned our attention, therefore, to the residents of the state training schools.

In short, we suspected that the diagnosis of cultural-familial (or educable, origin unknown, and so on) *mental retardation* was to the child what the diagnosis of *mental illness* (functional psychosis) was to the adult: a myth which conveniently and effectively serves society, enabling it to misconstrue completely the nature of its needed reforms.

As social scientists we translated our concern and our hunches into a set of interrelated hypotheses, conducted extensive research in two large state schools and several smaller institutions for the mentally retarded, analyzed and examined the results, and, finally, wrote this report.

Rather than an exhaustive review of the mental retardation literature (see Robinson & Robinson, 1966), in the first chapter we present some of the prevalent conceptions and theories of mental retardation, stressing the problems that beset them. Following the linguistic and logical criticisms of these theories, we outline a new way to conceptualize retardation, one which we use throughout the book. Chapter 2 describes the characteristics of the youngsters we used in our studies as well as those of the institutions in which the subjects reside. The next four chapters comprise the substantive portion of the book—the research. In Chapter 3 we are con-

cerned primarily with the manipulative tactics of mental retardates.
We focus here on the retardates' use, in experimental settings, of
impression management as an interpersonal strategy by which they
attempt to satisfy their primary motivations. We explore the relationship between in-experimental behavior of the retardates and
their ways of adapting to their everyday environment, the training
school. Of particular interest are the styles of adaptation that the
retardates evolve in the course of their stay in the institution, patterns of activities that show exactly to what extent retardates can
control their own lives. Chapter 5 deals with the comparison between the retardates' attitudes toward mental retardation, the institution, its staff, and life in general, and the attitudes of the staff.
In Chapter 6 family background information—taken from the social
caseworkers' records—of the children we studied is presented. The
reasons for the incarceration of the retardates supplied by the social workers are counterbalanced by the reasons given by the retardates themselves. The data chapters are sequenced so that an
ever-increasing segment of the retardates' behavior and environment is available for examination: in Chapter 3, they are seen in
experimental situations; in Chapter 4, their everyday institutional
milieu is the setting; in Chapter 5, they are examined in the context of their conflict with the staff; and in Chapter 6, the setting
is the outside community prior to their incarceration.

In the final chapter, Chapter 7, we consider the theoretical, research, and treatment implications of the findings in the context
of our model. Here we address the professional and examine his
role in the social sanitation process, encouraging a new base of
operation for his professional activities. The recommendations for
treatment, which are radically at variance with current policy, emphasize the need to establish special communities not only for
mental retardates but for the others in the human community who
are unneeded or unwanted.

Since this book represents a truly collaborative effort on the part
of the authors, there is no senior or junior author; the names appear instead on a rotational basis. Most of the research presented
in the book was conducted while Benjamin Braginsky was a research staff psychologist at Yale University (under HEW grant
HDO 30008-01).

We would like to acknowledge our indebtedness to the admin-
istrators, the staff, and especially to the residents of the training
schools in which we conducted our research. In addition, we would
like to express our appreciation to our friends and colleagues who

read the manuscript and who gave thoughtful suggestions concerning it: Drs. Jules Holzberg, Elizabeth Ring, and Alexander Tolor. For their assistance in data collection and analyses we wish to thank Alan Church, Sandra Dudley, Myles Edwards, Martin Grosse, James McAuley, Ellen Rakusin, and Carl Sachs. For typing the manuscript our appreciation goes to Anna Braginsky, Theresa Delco, Ann Esposito, and Ona Langer. We would like to acknowledge the help of Theodore Sarbin, the consulting editor, in the preparation of our final manuscript, and the able assistance of Jeanette Ninas Johnson, who has seen our manuscript to press. We especially want to acknowledge Kenneth Ring, a colleague whose suggestions are always intelligent, provocative, and invaluable.

And an especially warm thank-you is in order to our families, who encouraged and facilitated the preparation of this manuscript.

D.D.B.
B.M.B.

New Haven, Conn.
November 1970

Contents

Once upon a time there dwelt on the outskirts of a large forest a poor woodcutter with his wife and two children; the boy was called Hansel and the girl Gretel. They had always little enough to live on, and once, when there was a great famine in the land, the woodcutter could not even provide them with daily bread.

One night, as he was tossing about in bed, full of cares and worry, he sighed and said to his wife, "What is to become of us? How are we to support our poor children, now that we have nothing more left even for ourselves?"

"Early in the morning," answered the woman, who was the children's stepmother, "we will take Hansel and Gretel out into the thickest part of the woods. There we shall light a fire for them, give them each a piece of bread and go on to our work, leaving them alone. They will not be able to find their way home, and we shall thus be rid of them."

"No, wife," said her husband, "that I won't do. How could I find it in my heart to leave my children alone in the woods? The wild beasts would come and tear them to pieces."

"Oh," said she, "then we must all four die of hunger, and you may just as well go and prepare the boards for our coffins." And she left him no peace till he had consented.

From *Hansel and Gretel*

A Day in the Life
of the Mentally Retarded

NAME: *Ruby James*   AGE: *16*   SEX: *Female*
LENGTH OF TIME IN TRAINING SCHOOL: *2 years*
DIAGNOSIS: *Mild retardation*

Q. How do you usually spend your day here?

A. Well, I work in the hospital so I get up at 5:30 in the morning. I have breakfast around 6 where I work. I work from 6 to 12:30 and from 1 until 3 I work in the workshop. Then I come back to the building and just rest until suppertime. After supper I don't do much, just talk to the girls until bedtime.

Q. What do you girls do in the building?

A. Sometimes we smoke, sometimes we listen to records and dance. We watch TV. Sometimes we just sit and talk to each other or chase around the dormitory.

Q. What do you do on weekends?

A. I work from 6 to 3 on Saturday. I work Sunday morning and have Sunday afternoon off. I don't have a full day off. When I'm off, I get my clothes ready for the dance on Saturday night. The dance is from 7 to 9.

Q. Why are you here?

A. Well, this is a long story—do you want to hear it? Well, this happened when I was home and my brother—I had trouble with my brother. Well, he got me pregnant. He is seventeen. I had the baby, but the baby passed away. The baby died and I was so unhappy. I thought the baby would live. My mother was glad that the baby died, but I felt bad. She blamed me and I blamed her and I got all mixed up and she blamed me for everything. When I came here, she told the building charge that she really didn't blame me, but it was my real mother's fault.

Q. Do you have a father?

A. I don't know where he is. I guess he lives in Neuville with my sister; but my mother died when I was twelve years old. She died of a heart attack.

Q. How old were you when you had the baby?

A. I was thirteen. I was living with a foster mother. She blamed me. It was my stepbrother that made me pregnant. When I got out of the hospital—I was there just a week— they called the school and told the superintendent why I had to come here and he said okay. So I came here. A lot of girls come here when they are pregnant—but I wasn't.

Q. How long have you been here?

A. Almost three years. I did pretty good in school before I came here. But the boys kept bothering me in junior high.

I hate boys. They ask me to go with them, but I say no. I still have a boyfriend here.

Q. What would you be doing if there wasn't a place like this?

A. I wouldn't know.

Q. Are there any good things about being in here?

A. No. I don't like most of my girl friends. Don't like this place. Every time we go on trips somewhere, swimming in the summertime or shopping, the people always look at us and we feel so bad to go on these trips. We don't want the people to look at us. They know we are from the school. We don't like to go anywhere, especially outside the school.

Q. Do you consider yourself retarded?

A. No. But I heard a lot of people saying we are retarded. But us big, bright girls are not really retarded. Maybe they are talking about the small ones like in the hospital wing. But us bright girls are not retarded and I don't know how come they call us retarded.

Q. How does it make you feel when they call you retarded?

A. Well, I just get up and walk away and say the same thing to them—you are retarded.

Q. What is this place for?

A. Well, it's a place for kids who run away or something like that. Some kids get into trouble by boys.

Q. If you could, would you leave this place tomorrow?

A. And go where? I wouldn't know where to go. I would have to know where I would go.

Q. Are there any kids here who try to make people think that they are stupid when they are really bright?

A. Yes. I saw some like that.

Q. Are there any girls here as bright as some of the attendants?

A. There are girls in this building that are as bright as some of the attendants. Some are pretty bright. Some are brighter than the attendants.

Q. Why are they here?

A. Well, some are here because they have been bad and some are here because they have mean mothers who don't take care of them, hit them and everything like that.

Q. Are there some people who have been in here for a long time who like it here and who don't want to leave?

A. Yeah. You're telling me they do. I guess some of the kids like it here. I just wonder why they won't let us bright girls out and go on parole and live with foster parents that either don't have any boys or just have girls? We are bright enough to know what to do and we could go outside and find jobs or something. But some of us girls want to get out and get married. Some of the attendants said that you can't get married when you go out, but I knew this girl and boy who used to be here and both of them went on parole and got married. How come they don't let us bright girls out? I have been good so far since I've been here. I've had a lot of things happen in my life. I would rather be in a hospital than in this place. I was in a hospital for two months when I was twelve years old. It was better than this. I got into an accident with my mother and father. My sister went through a car window and she died in the hospital. My mother had to have three operations. I've had hard times.

NAME: *Timothy Peck*   AGE: *10*   SEX: *Male*
LENGTH OF TIME IN TRAINING SCHOOL: *1 year*
DIAGNOSIS: *Mild retardation*

Q. How do you typically spend your time during the week?

A. I get up at 6:30. At 7 o'clock I get to breakfast. Sometimes before, sometimes right on the hour. Then I go in my ward and do work that I am supposed to do. And then when I'm done, I sit down and look at TV, uh, television, whatever you call it. At 8:30 I have to get up and go to school until 3 o'clock, as usual. We go back to the ward and half of us boys work down in the dining room. We all stay and work for the, you know. I volunteer, but they have some regular workers. I help them out before supper, if they need the help. If they don't before supper and they do after, I'd be pleased to help them out.

Q. Well, then what do you do?

A. After we eat, after all the work is, after everything is all done, we go back and take a shower around 5 or a quarter after or something like that. We sit down and watch TV for the rest of the night. And talk until the aide wants somebody to do the work.

Q. What do you do on weekends?

A. Oh, we horse around until it's time for us to go to the movies. That's at a quarter after 8.

Q. At night?

A. No. In the morning on Saturday. On Friday, at night. The movies are finished at 10:30 on Saturday morning and 9 o'clock Friday night. After, oh, we sit in the ward and talk 'til they call us for lunch and then after lunch I go in the ward, brush my teeth and sit down and watch TV until suppertime. If there ain't nothing much on, they'll open—we have an exit door—and they'll open the door and go outside. We use it to go outside and play. We'll play outside, if we don't want to see TV. It's up to the aide in charge of the ward. We usually stay in. They keep the door closed and locked, 'cause they don't want us outside. Then after supper we take showers and stay on the ward and watch television, and if we want to, the aide will pick some boys to do the work. We'll stay up a little later. We go to bed at 8:30. We usually go to bed at 9 o'clock on weekends. Every day it should be, but they put us to bed sometimes at 7.

Q. Tim, why are you here at the training school?

A. Oh, I'm here for destructing things—destructing things on the outside. Breaking rules in the house and things like that.

Q. Who brought you here?

A. A social worker from the social service from the Juvenile Court.

Q. Did your mother and father want you to come?

A. I have a mother, but I don't have a father. Before I came here he stayed where we used to live before. My mother she lives off the state now. She used to try to get a job and everything. She really didn't want me to come here. She didn't want me to come here. She didn't know which school I was gonna come to anyway until they sent me here. I didn't want to come, but I had to. I made one mistake. Anyway, I came without my mother. Usually when a kid goes to a school he should go with his mother. They put me here, they were supposed to put me in the Neighborhood Center a little closer to my house.

Q. What would you be doing if you weren't here?

A. Oh well, I don't know what I'd be doing.

Q. Are there any good things about being here?

A. Before you say that, I do know what I'd be doing. Exactly. Doing the same thing that I just told you—destructing things that you're not supposed to. Going on to things like tracks, you know, train tracks and things like that that I used to go on. What I did that summer when I was home.

Q. Are there any good things about being in a place like this?

A. Well, there's not too many good things over here. There's things that I don't like sometimes. I don't like some of the boys, you know, how they come after me and try to beat me up and everything.

Q. What's this place for?

A. I don't know why they built it. I think I have a little hint why they built it. For kids so they won't be put in an asylum, a cell, like jail.

Q. Do you consider yourself to be retarded?

A. Not for real.

Q. What about most of the boys in the building?

A. I would consider a few, not too many.

Q. Well, why do you think that they are here?

A. Well, I don't know why, but I consider a few of them that's retarded. At least they could really try to help themselves and at least something. The others, well maybe some of them might be here 'cause their mothers wants to go on a very long vacation or something like that. And they don't want the boys around. So they put them in the school until they come back. If some of them had to come up with the mother, she'd have to put the kid in the school so that he won't be in her way.

Q. Have you ever seen anyone here act stupid even though he isn't?

A. Yeah. Say somebody is trying to get you out and you say stupid things, they might not even let you out. They won't let you out, if you keep saying things like that. The stupider you act, they won't let you out. If a boy wants to get out, he'll act the way he is supposed to be. He'll just sit on that chair and watch TV 'til somebody comes up and asks him, "Could you do me a favor?", then he'll go do it.

Q. Say somebody likes it here and wants to stay, then what would he do?

A. Well, as far as I know they won't let him out, but if they want to stay, all they got to do is goof up at home again.

Q. Are there any boys here as bright as the aides?

A. There is a lot of them that's ten times brighter than one aide, than a dozen aides that work here.

Q. Do they show how bright they really are?

A. No. Half of them just sit down on their chair. I'm the only one, just about the only one, in the ward that shows my respect for an aide. I'll say this, there's another boy in the dining room that shows respect. It's a good thing to show an aide you're bright—when he wants you to do something, do it for him. If you show him your respect and everything like that, they think you ain't as stupid as you are. They will like you very much. They'll take a chance on taking you home for maybe a weekend, or something like that, a short vacation.

Q. How do the aides expect you to behave?

A. They say I am emotionally retarded. They said I was retarded, but in a way I'm not, you know, in a way you're half stupid and half not. Well, in a way one boy will be stupid and in a way another boy will be bright. You see, what they say about me over here when my mother asks them, "Is this boy emotionally disturbed or is he retarded?" Well, the one that takes care of the office, he'll say, "Your boy is retarded in a way, he is retarded in a way that he can help himself, not emotionally retarded, not emotionally disturbed." I don't agree with it at all. I'm over here really just to show respect and learn things like that.

CHAPTER

1

Mental Retardation:
A Defective Concept

There are few sights more pitiful than the children who live in institutions for the mentally retarded. The feeling is inescapable when one sees the profoundly retarded inmates, incapacitated, needing almost total care. Yet it is, perhaps, more acute at the sight of the mildly retarded child. One's pity for the profoundly retarded is tempered somehow by the obvious nature of their defects, and one is relieved that institutions exist which assume this human burden. When one, however, encounters thousands and thousands of mildly retarded children living in the same institutions, children who in many ways so much resemble children on the outside, the pity is compounded with confusion. It is this group of mentally retarded children, the cultural-familial, educable, unknown-origin retardates (or whatever they happen to be called at a particular institution), rather than the profoundly and severely brain-damaged or genetically impaired persons, with whom this book is concerned.

The similarity between these retarded children and normal children has often led the uninitiated, nonprofessional observer to ask: Why are these children incarcerated? Why must they live in institutions rather than at home? What exactly is *wrong* with them? These queries are not unlike the ones to which the experts have addressed themselves. In particular, the last question has gained the attention of specialists from many disciplines, all attempting to delineate exactly what is *wrong* with the mildly retarded.

WHAT IS MENTAL RETARDATION?

For centuries, plagued by the problem of defining mental retardation, men have made innumerable clinical observations, and, more recently, have conducted thousands of empirical studies. Yet we are no closer to an answer than were the ancient Greeks. "The casual observer," comments Kanner (1948), "may be forgiven for feeling puzzled at the groping of men and women deservedly acknowledged as experts. It does indeed seem strange that after nearly a century of scientific occupation with 'feeble-mindedness' those best informed should still be wondering what they have been, and are dealing with [pp. 36–37]."

And yet this lack of conceptual clarity has not prevented the American Association of Mental Deficiency (Heber, 1959) from estimating that 5½ million persons in this country are afflicted with mental retardation, nor the President's Panel on Mental Retardation (1962) from ranking it fourth in prevalence among all diseases. There must, then, be some definition in mind for those persons computing prevalence rates. And, as Heber (1962) laments, there are probably too many definitions in too many minds:

> We have definitions cast in the language of the psychiatrist, neurologist, pediatrician, geneticist, sociologist, psychologist and

educator. Many of these definitions are at variance with one another. Volumes of the *American Journal of Mental Deficiency* are replete with statements expounding the merits or demerits of various concepts of retardation [p. 70].

The buzzing state of confusion described by Kanner seems to be the result, then, not of a lack of definitions but rather of too many definitions. The use of the term "mental retardation" by the President's Panel on Mental Retardation (1962) offers a striking example of—as well as a clue to the reason for—the conceptual chaos in this area. First the Panel uses mental retardation to denote an *actual disease entity:* "Mental retardation ranks as a major national health, social and economic problem—it afflicts twice as many individuals as blindness, polio, cerebral palsy, and rheumatic heart disease, combined." Then, unlike the diseases to which it has just been compared, the President's Panel proceeds to use the term as a *culturally relative concept:* "Because mental retardation is a relative concept depending on the prevailing educational and cultural standards, there is no completely satisfactory measure of mental retardation." Surely, rheumatic heart disease is rheumatic heart disease whether the afflicted has a college degree or not, whether he is from the ghetto or Park Avenue. Finally, the Panel denies altogether the "realness" of mental retardation (be it as a disease entity or a culturally relative concept) by using it as a *hypothetical construct.* Specifically, mental retardation is presented as a construct that links a multitude of antecedent conditions with behavioral outcomes such as low intelligence: "The term 'mental retardation' is a simple designation for a group of complex phenomena stemming from many different causes, but one key common characteristic found in all cases is *inadequately developed intelligence.*"

The conceptual confusion outlined above somehow seems unimportant in the light of this last disclosure by the Panel (the universal "key common characteristic"). What does it matter whether mental retardation is a hypothetical construct, a relative concept, or a disease entity, if we can identify with certainty all mentally retarded persons by their "inadequately developed intelligence"? But can we? Another group of experts, Delay, Pichot, and Perse (1952) believe, to the contrary, that *adequate intelligence does not preclude mental retardation.* According to these authors (and they are not alone) a good intelligence quotient may be merely a ruse to hide social incompetence. Thus, socially incompetent persons with adequate IQ scores are seen as being afflicted with "camouflaged mental deficiency."

Furthermore, a severe blow to any potential meaning that might reside in the concept of retardation is dealt by Robinson and Robinson (1965) when they state:

> . . . mental retardation is only a symptom and not a syndrome. If a child is functioning at a retarded level, then he is retarded, for the time being at least, whether this symptom is associated with a permanent organic damage, with transient illness, with a familial disorder, with cultural deprivation, or with psychosis [p. 226].

Accordingly, mental retardation is a symptom, yet to be described, that can be associated with anything and everything, permanently or temporarily.

In short, the students of mental retardation cannot offer a reliable or valid definition of this term. And yet we find that this disquieting state of affairs hardly deters these perspicacious men and women from classifying and diagnosing individuals as mentally retarded, prescribing treatment for them, constructing vast institutions to house them, and developing rehabilitation programs for them. Surely, the time and effort expended on these activities as well as that for computing prevalence rates and conducting extensive research to find the causes of this "affliction" *must* be predicated in the belief that mental retardation is a *real* illness, rather than an inadequately defined construct (although lip-service is paid to the latter notion).

In order to better understand, as we feel we must, the behavior and belief system of these specialists, we shall briefly explore the thought processes that enable people to accept as real something that may not exist.

THE MAKING OF A MYTH

The experts' failure to reject the notion of mental retardation or to seriously question its utility is not only abetted by coddling untestable definitions, but also by refusing to acknowledge the rules of logic. Thus, most experts *assume* the validity of the concept while they set out to demonstrate it. Rather than asking first whether retardation is a meaningful or "real" entity, they ask, "How can we demonstrate that retardates are different from normals?" An illicit conclusion, therefore, is entertained (that retardation exists) before it has been adequately defined and empirically demonstrated.

Skinner (1953) and Sarbin (1967) describe the processes that allow the professional as well as the man on the street to accept the "realness" of something for which there may be no referent (also see Bijou, 1966). This phenomenon is particularly common with respect to psychological "characteristics." As Skinner (1953) has pointed out:

> Trait names usually begin as adjectives—"intelligent", "aggressive", "disorganized", "angry", "introverted", and so on, but the almost inevitable linguistic result is that adjectives give birth to nouns. The things to which these nouns refer are then taken to be the active causes of the aspects. We begin with "intelligent behavior", pass first to "behavior which shows intelligence" and then to "behavior which is the effect of intelligence." . . . But at no point in such a series do we make contact with an event outside of the behavior itself which justifies the claim of a causal connection [p. 202].

Skinner's analysis is particularly instructive here. We never directly observe mental retardation, or, for that matter, mentally retarded behavior. The term mental retardation is simply a metaphor chosen to connote certain assumed qualities of putative, invisible mental processes. More specifically, it is inferred that it appears *as if* retarded mental processes underlie particular behaviors. Or, we infer that behavior appears *as if* it were retarded. Too often the *as if* conditions are forgotten and we are left with "mentally retarded behavior." As a consequence, retardation becomes accepted as a concrete disease state instead of the metaphor that it is.

It is at this point that Sarbin (1967) would say that the concept has progressed through the "metaphor-to-myth" transformation. This cognitive strategy, according to Sarbin, takes the following form:

> Every metaphor contains a wealth of connotations, each connotation has the potential for manifold implications, and each implication is a directive to action. While metaphors are ordinarily used by people to facilitate communication, the peril is always at hand that people may be used by metaphors (Turbayne, 1960). Such a peril is activated when the user of a metaphor ignores, forgets, or purposely drops syntactical modifiers, such as *as if,* that denote the metaphor, and instead employs the word in literal fashion. To say "Jones is a saint" carries one set of implications if we supply the tacit modifier ("it is *as if* Jones is a saint"); the sentence carries a radically different set of implications if the predicate is treated as literal. The effects of permanently ignoring the metaphoric properties of a word, that is, of dropping the expressed or tacit modifiers, is to hypostatize an entity. Such hypostatization sets the stage for myth-making [p. 447].

And this, indeed, appears to be what the experts have created: a myth. Thus, despite the diffuseness of the definitions and the theoretical shambles concerning mental retardation, the specialists can carry on their jobs. The myth they have created, and over the years maintained, represents an almost *universally shared conception* about the nature of mental retardation, a conception which enables them to justify their activities.

THE "NATURE" OF MENTAL RETARDATION: THE MYTH

Despite the theoretical heterogeneity there appears to be a theme common to most students of mental retardation; that is, a shared conception concerning the nature of the affliction. As with all good myths, this shared conception is composed of an interrelated set of beliefs, virtually so self-evident that they are, for the most part, maintained without awareness.

The major component of the prevalent conception of mental retardation, to which we have alluded and which is so taken for granted that it has been almost invisible to scrutiny, is the belief that mental retardation is a *real internal pathological process,* as real as pneumonia or heart disease. The President's Panel (1962) discusses retardation as an enormous health problem afflicting so many individuals that "only four disabling conditions—mental illness, cardiac disease, arthritis, and cancer —have a higher prevalence." The public, in fact, has been applauded by Robinson and Robinson (1965) for finally recognizing mental retardation "for the magnitude of the *public health problem* it presents [italics ours]."

A second belief, intimately related to the first, is that persons afflicted with mental retardation are not only different from other persons but are less than human, existing at some point lower on the phylogenetic scale than the rest of mankind. In short, mentally retarded persons are seen as defective human organisms. The "defective orientation" to mental retardation, as Zigler (1966) has pointed out, is merely a contemporary version of the old degeneration theory of behavior deviancy. The degeneration theory, presented in 1857 by Morel, concluded that all varieties of mental disorders, including insanity and mental deficiency, are related. Moreover, he proposed that all deviations from the normal human type that are transmitted by heredity be considered degenerations.

In tracing this history of today's variants of the degeneration theory, Zigler (1966a) reports:

> The defect orientation to mental retardation originally emphasized the notion of moral defect and stemmed anywhere from the belief that retardates were possessed by a variety of devils to the empirical evidence of their exhibiting an inordinately high incidence of socially unacceptable behaviors, such as crime and illegitimacy [p. 108].

At the turn of the century, Fernald (1912), a pioneer in this field, was unabashedly explicit in articulating the moral defects of the mentally retarded:

. . . the feebleminded are a parasitic, predatory class, never capable of self-support or of managing their own affairs. The great majority ultimately become public charges in some form. They cause unutterable sorrow at home and are a menace and danger to the community. Feebleminded women are almost invariably immoral. We have only begun to understand the importance of feeblemindedness as a factor in the causation of pauperism, crime and other social problems. . . . Every feebleminded person, especially the high grade imbecile, is a potential criminal, needing only the proper environment and opportunity for the development and expression of his criminal tendencies. The unrecognized imbecile is a most dangerous element in the community [pp. 90–91].

The specific defect that was believed to set the mentally retarded apart from the rest of humanity, then, was their lack of intelligent or good judgment. "Moral judgment," said Terman (1916), "like business judgment, social judgment, or any other kind of higher thought process, is a function of intelligence. Morality cannot flower and fruit if intelligence remains infantile [p. 11]." Accordingly, Terman maintained "that every feebleminded woman is a potential prostitute."

The same beliefs, albeit more disguised and sophisticated in presentation, still can be seen in contemporary descriptions of the retarded. Today, as in the past, retardates represent the embodiment of ignorance, incompetence, and ineffectuality. In Benda's (1954) terms, the retardate is "a person who is incapable of managing himself or his affairs, or being taught to do so, and who requires supervision, control, and care for his own welfare and the welfare of the community [p. 1115]." Similarly, Heber (1962) depicts the typical behavior associated with mental retardation as:

. . . behavior which does not meet the standards of dependability, reliability, and trustworthiness; behavior which is persistently asocial, antisocial, and/or excessively hostile. . . . inability to recognize the needs of other persons in interpersonal interactions . . . inability to delay gratification of needs and lack of long range goal striving or persistence with response only to short term goals [p. 77].

More recently, as Zigler (1966a) notes, there has been a shift away from emphasis on moral defects; the emphasis is now being placed upon "defects in either physical or cognitive structures. . . . Whatever the ontogenesis, the defect position emphasizes the innate, if not immutable, difference between retardates and normals [pp. 108–109]." A partial list supplied by Zigler of some of the innate defects attributed to retardates includes:

1. Impermeability of the boundaries between regions in cognitive structure (Kounin, 1941a; 1941b; Lewin, 1936).

2. Malfunctioning disinhibitory mechanisms (Siegel and Foshee, 1960).

3. Improper development of the verbal system resulting in a dissociation between verbal and motor systems (Luria, 1956; O'Connor and Hermelin, 1959).

4. Inadequate neural satiation related to brain modifiability of cortical conductivity (Spitz, 1963).

5. Relative brevity in the persistence of the stimulus trace (Ellis, 1963).

6. Primary and secondary rigidity caused by subcortical and cortical malfunctions (Goldstein, 1943).

This list of defects seems to have, to a large degree, face validity when we encounter those persons with massive neurological damage which renders them profoundly disabled, as well as those persons with known morphological imperfections, such as mongolism. This group, however, comprises only about 20 percent of all persons diagnosed as mentally retarded. For the remaining 80 percent who have no verifiable or noticeable organic/genetic impairment, the list of defects appears to be inapplicable. That is, for the cultural-familial (or educable, origin-unknown, and so on), the defect orientation appears to have no validity.

The largest group of retardates, the cultural-familials, appear, in fact, so much like normal persons that Robinson and Robinson (1965) were prompted to describe them as:

> . . . lacking the gross physical handicaps or dramatic symptoms of the pathologic syndromes. . . . They often seem to be developing in a rather normal intellectual pattern which is remark-

able primarily for its slowness. Most of these children could pass cursory inspection without seeming to differ blatantly from their age mates [p. 208].

The cultural-familial group, therefore, presents a major threat to the belief system underlying the concept of retardation. Since this group does not meet the criteria which typically define mental retardation, how then are they diagnosed and separated from the rest of humanity? What methods other than a cursory examination do the experts employ?

In order to illustrate the difficulties encountered by the diagnostician, we shall, for the moment, accept the American Association of Mental Deficiency's (Heber, 1959) definition and beliefs about familial retardation. According to this austere organization, the requirements that must be met for this diagnostic label are: (a) the child must be mildly retarded with (b) no indication of a cerebral pathologic condition, and (c) there must be evidence of retarded intellectual functioning in at least one of the parents and in one or more of the brothers or sisters of the child in question.

Yet if one accepts this definition one is beset with almost insurmountable problems. Sarason (1969) very succinctly describes them:

> The assessment of intellectual functioning can be made only through tests or procedures that reflect a comprehensive theory of intelligence—a condition not met by the most frequently used tests today. . . . It cannot be too strongly stated that most of our tests are woefully inadequate for the evaluation of various human aptitudes. . . . Despite the work and writings of Guilford and others (Sarason and Gladwin, 1958) it is still unfortunately the case that assessment of intellectual functioning and the diagnosis of mental subnormality are based on tests which tap a very restricted sample of intellectual functions or processes. . . . Fulfilling the criteria for the diagnosis of mental retardation . . . encounters more than the obstacle of inadequate tests or the inadequate use of conventional tests. An equally thorny obstacle is . . . our failure and inability to focus and assess the level and quality of problem-solving behavior *outside the test situation.* . . . The third problem is of a much more practical nature, i.e.

assessing the intellectual functioning of parents and sibs. In actual practice the appropriate kind of data are frequently not available, and even if we were disposed to obtain these data one would run into understandable resistance on the part of the parents who, like so many of us, do not look kindly on having one's "brain" examined [pp. 50–59].

In short, an amazing situation exists wherein specialists are measuring, with inadequate and inappropriate devices, a concept which has yet to be reliably and validly defined.

Thus, the advocates of the mental retardation point of view are in a logically and empirically untenable position; a position more untenable, perhaps, than those who once proposed that the earth was flat. The belief that the earth was flat had, at least, some denotable and visible referent; everyone knew what "flat" meant, and everyone could see for themselves the "flatness" of the earth. But more importantly, this belief lent itself to empirical verification or rejection. Although these rather rudimentary supports for belief maintenance are absent for the proponents of mental retardation, the strength of their beliefs does not appear to languish. Instead, we find that the metaphor, "mental retardation," is treated as possessing "thingness," a concrete, corporeal existence, making it almost impossible to dislodge from the advocates' system of beliefs; one rarely rejects the experience of "things."

And yet, as we have noted, specialists very often do notice that retardates act in ways contrary to how they are "supposed to" behave. How then can the experts maintain their beliefs (sometimes called theory) when reality suggests that their theories are misleading, misconstrued representations; when reality suggests massive reorganization or total abandonment of the belief system?

MAINTAINING THE MYTH

Once established, myths (like any system of beliefs) tend to perpetuate themselves. Even when contradictory data are observed (for example, retardates can pass for normal children), the myth guarantees its existence by assimilating the contrary data. Historians of science (Conant, 1947, and Kuhn, 1962) have proposed that in themselves counter-instances are not sufficient to cause a belief system to be discarded, or, in fact, even to be revised.

Because what is legitimatized as scientific fact is, to a large extent, dictated by the belief system itself, and since all belief systems outlaw observations which would be recognized by others, little thought is required in maintaining a myth; the theory does it for you. Kuhn (1962) describes clearly the fate of data not in keeping with one's theory: "Assimilating a new sort of fact demands a more than additive adjustment of theory, and until that adjustment is completed—until the scientist has learned to see nature in a different way—the new fact is not quite a scientific fact at all [p. 53]."

With respect to beliefs concerning mental retardation, assimilation of counter-data takes a specific form. Since the belief that most needs to be preserved (because it represents the underpinning of the conception of retardation) is that retardates are "defective" human organisms, any data that would imply that retardates can function in a similar manner, and, particularly, in a superior way to normals would *have to* be reinterpreted or ignored. To illuminate the process of counter-instance reinterpretation in the area of mental retardation, only a few examples will be presented (although the literature is replete with examples).

As we mentioned earlier, both Kounin (1941a,b) and Lewin (1936) believed that retardates have impermeable boundaries between regions in their cognitive structures. A correlated hypothesis is that retardates would exhibit greater rigidity in thought processes than normals (Kounin, 1943; Lewin, 1936). In a study conducted by Osborn (1960) a clustering task was designed in order to test this assumption by combining and organizing concepts. Contrary to expectations, the results indicated that both the organic and familial retardates functioned as well as the normal group. Moreover, on some of the tasks, the trend (although not statistically significant) was in the direction of superiority of the retardates over the normals.

Rather than finding rigidity and impoverishment in conceptual functioning, Osborn found that retardates had "pronounced peaks and valleys of functioning [p. 356]."

Yet despite the surprising performance of the retardates in comparison to normals, the conclusion focused on the similarity in performance of the organic and familial retardates:

> Results of this study suggest that functional disorder in the mild retardate may be at least as important as structural impairment in determining intellectual development. . . . These results imply that the retardate is *unable to function to the limits of his capacity* even when dealing with materials or situations with which he has had ample experience (as in the present experiment) [p. 356; italics ours].

The author thus totally ignores the data which showed that normals performed worse on some tasks, and certainly no better than the retardates on others. By doing this Osborn is able to maintain his belief in retardate "deficiency" and "ineffectuality"; the myth is preserved.

If we, however, were to accept his logic, and if the author pursued it with the remainder of these data, we would have to conclude that normal subjects are even more impaired and less able to function to the limits of their capacity than the retardates. This conclusion, not surprisingly, was not articulated by Osborn.

Richman, Kellner, and Allen (1968), confronted with the embarrassing findings that organic retardates were more accurate than familial retardates, who in turn were more accurate than normals in their judgments of size constancy, try to salvage their theory in the following manner:

> The findings of greater size constancy among organics than among familial retardates or normal adolescents is somewhat surprising. It is possible that the superior veridicality of the brain-injured S's in this investigation may be partly explained in terms of Werner's (1948) concept of *"developmental arrest."*
> . . . It is clear that organic retardates (and to a lesser extent, familial retardates) exhibit a relative lack of conceptual func-

tioning and thus remain somewhat fixated at the sensory-motor and/or perceptual level of cognitive development. It is also conceivable, however, that within these more *"primitive" areas of intellectual functioning,* and in particular, the area of perceptual-motor operations . . . that a *lack of subordination to higher-level, conceptual operations* is accompanied by a greater differentiation and refinement of available perceptual response patterns in organic retardates [pp. 581–582; italics ours].

According to this interpretation, the unexpected superiority in performance of the organic and familial retardates was the result of a putative lack of a high-order conceptual system. Accuracy in the perception of size constancy, previously regarded as a psychological asset, is now seen as a consequence of a psychological deficit. To uphold the myth, the authors must transform the retardates' *ability* into a *liability.*

In areas other than research, the assimilative function of beliefs can also be observed. An obvious threat in the theoretical realm must also, in order to keep the faith, be disposed of. One such example is the concept of "pseudo-feeblemindedness" (Arthur, 1947; Benton, 1956; Kratter, 1959; Kanner, 1948), which simply refers to the diagnosis of a child as retarded when, in fact, he is not—a less than rare phenomenon (see Sarason, 1969).

Papageorgis (1963), in a position paper, argues against this concept.

Pseudo-feeblemindedness is invoked when a person previously classified as feebleminded, or mentally retarded, on the basis of some criterion or criteria, no longer appears so upon re-evaluation (Hutt & Gibby, 1958). The existence of this notion has at least two clear implications. First, by questioning the earlier diagnosis, it is assumed that mental retardation diagnoses should be correct prognoses as well. Stated in other terms, it is necessary for mental retardation, in order to be real, to be permanent (Doll, 1940). This situation can arise if we also *mistake performance* for *capacity.* It is the contention of this paper that it is quite meaningful to distinguish diagnosis from prognosis, and that, consequently, there is nothing amiss in considering a case of well-diagnosed mental retardation "cured" and thus avoid the mental gymnastics needed to challenge the validity of the previously obtained performance sample. At a given time, and at a given place, a person may or may not function as a retardate. At a later time, in a different setting, and sometimes under different criteria, the same individual again may or may not function as a retardate [p. 342; italics ours].

Now, according to Papageorgis, a person can be retarded, then "cured," then retarded, then "cured," and so on. He can be retarded in setting A, and not in setting B; and, at a later time, he may become retarded in setting B, and cured in setting A. If we were to accept his proposal, the concept of mental retardation could *never* be challenged—a state of affairs that would, no doubt, please many advocates, but that would result in utter chaos. Considering the shortcomings of even the best tests of "intelligence," and the rarity of "cures," it is amazing that the author rejects completely the most logical, obvious and parsimonious explanation of the differences that might be found between two IQ scores for the same person (in particular, where test score 1 is lower than test score 2): namely, that the first test was an inaccurate measure, providing an unfair assessment of the person's "intellectual functioning." This explanation, however simple, would not fit comfortably with the traditional beliefs concerning retardation.

There are, fortunately, others in this field who have recognized the serious flaws and gross inadequacies inherent in the traditional conception, especially with respect to cultural-familial retardation. As a result, several authors have attempted to modify or replace some of the commonly held assumptions.

THE SEARCH FOR ALTERNATIVES TO THE MYTH: SOCIAL PARADIGMS

The theme common to those who have questioned the prevalent conception of mental retardation is their opposition to the innateness of the disorder and their emphasis instead upon societal standards and social pressures as major determinants in the classification of a person as retarded. Here too, however, there is divergence: some maintain that these factors produce the intellectual *deficit;* others, although rejecting the defect orientation, stress the motivational and emotional *differences* between retardates and normals; still others (the present authors included) *reject* altogether the notion of differences as well as the concept of mental retardation.

Kanner's (1948) description of the "pseudo-feebleminded" represents clearly the first point of view:

> The members of this group are not truly and absolutely feeble-minded or *mentally* deficient. Their principal shortcoming is a greater or lesser degree of inability to comply with the *intellectual* requirements of their society. In other respects, they may be as mature or immature, stable or unstable, secure or insecure, placid or moody, aggressive or submissive as any other member of the species. The "deficiency" is an *ethnologically determined phenomenon* relative to the local standards and, even within those standards, relative to educational postulates, vocational ambitions, and family expectations. They are "subcultural" in our society but may not be even that in a different, less sophisticated setting [p. 374].

An example of the second divergent theme is afforded by Zigler and Harter (1969), who are explicit in rejecting the myth of retardate defectiveness:

> It is unfortunate that so little work emanating from a personality point of view has been done with the retarded. Some progress has been made, however, and much of the recent work supports the view that it is not necessary to employ constructs other than those used to account for the behavior of normal individuals in explaining the behavior of the familial retarded. It appears that many of the reported differences between retardates and normals of the same MA [mental age] are a result of motivational and emotional differences which reflect differences in environmental histories, and are not a function of innate deficiencies [p. 55].

In perhaps the strongest indictment against the prevalent conception, Brabner (1967) questions altogether the use of the term mental retardation:

. . . the concept of mental retardation, like the concept of mental illness, is a useless one for understanding and modifying non-adaptive behavior, primarily because the so-called "condition" of mental retardation is not an identifiable behavior entity. It is pointed out, further, that the relationship between subaverage general intellectual functioning and non-adaptive behavior is far from clear and that any "explanation" of such behavior in terms of intellectual criteria is simplistic. . . . Medical men, for convenience, will customarily toss various diseases of unknown etiology into one all-inclusive category, e.g. encephalitis, and gradually remove them from the category and reclassify them as they identify the etiological factors; gradually putting more of their professional house in order. When they identify phenylketonuria, for example, they haven't identified a form of mental retardation; they have identified an inborn metabolic error that produces many symptoms only one of which is subaverage general intellectual functioning. But for us as educators and psychologists to lump individuals in the petrifying categories we impose is presumptuous, unrevealing, unhelpful and confusing [p. 149].

Luria (1963) does not question the concept of cultural-familial retardation, but rather dismisses it entirely as a classification which is based solely on the "class bias" of our society —a bias aided and abetted by the "false theoretical principles of investigators." Mental retardation only has meaning for him when used to denote brain injury leading to anomalous development of mental activity.

Thus, there are a number of authors (also see Farber, 1968; Sarason, 1969), although clearly a minority in the field, who have criticized the underpinnings of the prevalent conception of mental retardation. The need for a new conception that will enable us to understand the children who become labeled "familial retardates" is obvious; but is there one available?

The potentials for an alternative conception or paradigm have been existent for a long time. These paradigmatic potentials may be found in a variety of areas embedded in the concepts of cultural deprivation, poverty, the sociological analysis of surplus populations, and so on. Some authors, many of whom agree and others who disagree with the concept of retardation, have hinted at or presented alternative models (for example, Zigler and Harter, 1969; Sarason, 1969; Farber, 1968; Mancuso and Dreisinger, 1969). Perhaps more important, paradigmatic alternatives have been suggested strongly by the already accumulated *data* of studies concerned with the epidemiology of retardation (we emphasize the data rather than the interpretation of these data generally offered by the retardation experts). The potential of these data has for the most part remained dormant, never fully explicated, overshadowed and obscured by the dominant conception of retardation.

Even Maher (1963), a proponent of the physicalistic view of intelligence, when he examined the social context surrounding the persons diagnosed as retarded, concluded:

> What constitutes mentally retarded behavior depends to a large extent upon the society which happens to be making the judgment. An individual who does not create a problem for others in his social environment and who manages to become self-supporting is usually not defined as mentally retarded no matter what his test IQ may be. Mental retardation is primarily a socially defined phenomenon, and it is in large part meaningless to speak of mental retardation without this criterion in mind [p. 230].

It is remarkable how so many students of mental retardation will agree with Maher's statement and still be blind to its implications. The literature on retardation is replete with instances of lip-service paid to this idea (see, for example, Kanner, p. 26). But what happens over and over is that the social factors deemed so vital are viewed solely in terms of their relationship to putative defects inside the retardate's head; not only intellectual defects, but emotional, interpersonal, motivational ones as well. The social variables, once assimilated into a defect model, are interpreted as etiological factors or "causes" of the deficiency, rather than being analyzed and understood in their own right. An example of how complex social factors can be transformed into "germs" which cause retardation is provided by Robinson and Robinson (1965):

> . . . few scientists today doubt that psychological factors can and often do have causal significance in many cases of mental

retardation. It seems abundantly clear that some circumstances are more favorable than others, that while most children grow up in situations which are on the whole conducive to their intellectual growth, others live in situations which *retard* or *stop* development in this sphere [p. 174].

Can social "germs" account for the dramatic variations found by age, sex, social class, community, and geographic area in the incidence of retardation (see Kanner, 1948; Ginzberg and Bray, 1953; Wunsch, 1951; U.S. Department of Health, Education and Welfare, 1963; Kirk and Weiner, 1959)? Or even more specifically, can they explain intelligently the data obtained by Ginzberg and Bray (1953) in their study of mental retardation among Army inductees? The rejection rate for Negroes in New England was 65 per 1000, while in the Southeast the rate was 202 per 1000; corresponding rates for whites in the same areas were 16 and 52 per 1000. Does this mean that there are a greater number of mental defectives residing in the Southeast than in New England, and especially defective Negroes?

By now it should be clear that the existing conception of mental retardation is inadequate, irrelevant, and a hindrance to understanding. It is not only desirable but indispensable, therefore, to replace this conception.

THE ONTOGENESIS OF A NEW PARADIGM

The basic assumptions underlying our paradigm—their genesis as well as a brief adumbration of the model itself—will be presented here. A fuller expression of our theoretical position and its implications for both research and action may be found in Chapter 7 following the presentation of our research findings.

First, we regard "mental retardation" as a crude metaphor, and we reject completely its reification to the status of an "illness of the mind." We do not believe (nor has it ever been demonstrated) that retardation is a real physical or intrapsychic state located somewhere in the heads of those who

Just calling not name calling / diagnosis

have been labeled "mentally retarded." Retardation exists, from our perspective, only to the extent that certain people persist in calling certain other people retarded. This name-calling or, more sophisticatedly, diagnosing is in itself an interesting phenomenon, offering a great deal of information concerning the people who label as well as the political and social forces that operate within our society. Unfortunately, it tells us almost nothing about those who are labeled "retarded."

Second, contrary to the dominant conceptions of the retarded which portray them as qualitatively dissimilar beings from the rest of us, our paradigm emphasizes just how human they are. What appears most blatantly erroneous to us is the picture of the retardate as a weak, ineffectual, inept, and stupid individual. We believe that the "retardate" has all the characteristics of ordinary human beings, and is, therefore, no more weak, ineffectual, inept, or stupid than most other people. Briefly, then, our conception of the nature of the retardate is in direct contradiction to the assumptions that are dominant today.

It should be noted at this point that initially our assumptions concerning the mentally retarded were not the outcome of formal or even informal observations leading to new insights into their behavior. The assumptions were derived, in fact, before we had any contact with retardates. Where then did these expectations come from? Simply, they were derived from an extensive program of research with a seemingly different "defective" population—hospitalized mental patients, especially schizophrenics (see Braginsky, Braginsky, and Ring, 1969). One outcome of our earlier work was the development of a conceptual model that had the potential to explain and predict the behavior of all persons considered functionally defective, regardless of the particular diagnostic label.

Before we present a summary of our findings with mental patients and examine their relevance to mental retardation, let us anticipate and attempt to reduce any discomfort that may arise by the introduction of the mentally ill into a discourse about the mentally retarded.

THE SIAMESE TWINS: MENTAL ILLNESS
AND MENTAL RETARDATION

The joining of two putative defects such as mental retardation and mental illness (namely schizophrenia) is not a heretical undertaking, since staunch traditionalists often have noted the amazing similarities that seem to exist between these groups with respect to etiology, dynamics, and the consequences of the "defects." Both concepts refer to assumed defects of the mind and, as such, they have been traditionally interpreted in the context of a medical model. As a result, both defects are assumed to be manifestations of some sort of recondite disease process, the manifestation being defined by the presence of some sort of deviant behavior.

There are other similarities to be drawn between these two "illnesses." For example, the retardate and the schizophrenic often are characterized in the same manner, typically being perceived as victims of their illnesses over which they have virtually no control. Intrapsychically and in their external, social affairs the retardate and the mentally ill person are conceived to be people *in whom* and *to whom* things happen; they are, accordingly, almost unable to be effective agents in determining their own fates. In general, they are both thought to be hopelessly and pathetically inadequate and ineffectual in pursuing rational goals.

We can, with the greatest of conceptual ease, substitute the term "retardate" for "chronic schizophrenic" in Schooler and Parkel's (1966) descriptive phrase: ". . . the chronic schizophrenic is not Seneca's "reasoning animal" or Spinoza's "social animal," or even a reasonably efficient version of Cassirer's symbol-using animal (p. 67)."

Moreover, a striking similarity exists between Heber's (1962) description of the mental defective presented before (see p. 18) and Redlich and Freedman's (1966) portrayal of the schizophrenic: "As the patient becomes deficient in discriminating his outer and inner realities, punitive, infantile, sexual, aggressive, and passive wishes, as well as fantasies and drives, gain prominence, surface to consciousness, and often appear uncontrolled [p. 464]."

Robinson and Robinson (1965), who more or less represent the traditional point of view, explicitly deal with mental illness and mental retardation under one conceptual roof:

> The high incidence of emotional disturbance among the retarded and conversely of mental retardation among the emotionally disturbed stems from a number of complex relationships between these two somewhat arbitrarily defined aspects of human behavior. In some instances it is likely that the two stem directly from the same causes, whether these are congenital defects, family relationships, or other conditions. . . . Early childhood psychoses . . . are associated with retardation in intellectual functioning. Such severe, intractable personality disorders almost by definition prevent the adequate development of verbal skills, abstract reasoning, and concept formation of the kind that is basic to the abilities which are called intelligence. Indeed, the coalescence of emotional and intellectual symptoms in childhood psychoses presents a very complex diagnostic situation. . . . In most cases, the diagnostic problem is not to discover whether emotional disturbance or mental retardation exists or even which came first, but rather to determine the depth and nature both of the child's emotional troubles and of his intellectual deficit. Many authors have pointed out the impossibility and the undesirability of attempting to separate emotional maladjustment from mental retardation in children. They contend that the total child responds to a stress or defect in any sphere of his life, and that most children therefore tend to show mixed symptoms in all spheres (Benda, Farrell and Chipman, 1961) [pp. 224–227].

Thus, from the perspective of those who believe in the concrete, independent existence of the two defects, both are perceived as interminably intertwined. Now let us turn to our research with the mentally ill and examine the results that enabled us to derive a set of expectations about the mentally retarded.

THE OUTLINES OF A NEW PARADIGM

The descriptive aspect of our research with the mentally ill primarily dealt with portraying the mental patient as he be-

haved both within and outside of the hospital, without resort-
ing to the various categories of psychiatric thought. On the
basis of a series of studies employing a variety of sociopsychological investigative techniques (experiments, interviews, questionnaires, attitude measurement, ecological analysis, and observations), evidence was uncovered that made it irrefutably
clear that the dominant conception of mental illness could not
account even for the most mundane activities of mental patients, much less for their complex "deviant" forms of behavior.
Not only was the psychiatric conception inadequate with
respect to explanatory power, but it precluded from obser-
vation the results of our studies.

For example, despite the belief that the mentally ill are hap-
less, acquiescent, and ineffectual persons, we found that they
were able to control to an amazing extent their fate in the
hospital. They were not only motivated to govern their own
lives, but they were successful as well. Moreover, the lives
that the mental patients chose for themselves were quite often
at variance with the therapeutic and rehabilitative goals of the
hospital, and, therefore, had to be carried out under the un-
suspecting noses of the staff—no easy task.

In their interactions with the staff, the mental patients were
able to manipulate the staff by creating the kinds of impressions (see Goffman, 1959) that would secure for them
otherwise unattainable benefits. Thus, when appropriate, the
patients would ingratiate themselves, or they would act at will
"crazy" or "healthy," whichever was more suited to the occasion in order to satisfy their needs and goals.

Aside from their displays of manipulativeness, they managed
to establish, within the confines of a large state institution,
personally gratifying, hedonic life styles—ones that were identical to their prehospital *weekend* styles of life. That is, how
a patient was accustomed to spending his leisure time before
entering the hospital was the best single predictor of how he
lived while in the hospital. If Mr. Jones, for instance, spent
his weekends socializing a good deal, his hospital life was
typified by this behavior; or, if Mrs. Smith before hospitalization spent her weekends loafing around the house, most of her
time was spent on the ward. The massive institutional setting

not only failed to overpower these purportedly helpless and deficient people, but the patients were resourceful enough to both subvert the therapeutic goals of and to exploit the hospital.

In short, we found, time and again, that mental patients acted in the hospital very much the way most of us act in the community—like ordinary human beings. They certainly did not act the way they were *supposed to.*

From these and other findings, the mentally ill patient emerged as a person who very often chooses (though not necessarily consciously) hospitalization as either an intermittent or an enduring way of life. As we have seen, in the institution he exploits his surroundings in an effective and rational manner, extracting from it personally satisfying outcomes. Although, at first, it seems somewhat peculiar that someone might choose to live his life in a mental hospital, closer examination showed that this is indeed a sensible choice. (It is this sensibility that became the cornerstone of the alternate paradigm to the traditional medical model.)

More specifically, if one examines the prehospital life of the people who become the "chronic schizophrenics," institutional life clearly has distinct advantages over societal membership. The characteristic common to most hard-core, chronic mental patients is their preinstitutional marginality (see Stearns and Ullman, 1949; Miller, 1967). They come from the ranks of the "under-class," the "unsettled" and "disreputable" poor, representing a population of misfits. They are people who find it difficult, and sometimes impossible, to cope with the continuously changing society in which we live. Every day they are confronted with their obsolescence and surplus value, feeling rejected and degraded. As the jetsam of swiftly changing society they have available one possibility—to find a way to *live outside* the mainstream of society.

The alternatives are few, but one prospect for those caught in such circumstances is to become a resident in a mental hospital. The costs of entering the fraternal order of the "mentally ill" are much less than the costs of despair and misery associated with their prehospital marginality. In such instances, to choose to "cop out" of this painful existence speaks of purposive, rational, and sensible behavior.

We do not mean to imply, however, that all mental patients are voluntary "cop outs." Some members of the unsettled poor eventually become residents through involuntary means, such as the "betrayal funnel" (see Goffman, 1961). Regardless of whether the mental patient first comes to the hospital because he wants to or because he is forced to, both entries represent facets of the same social phenomenon—"social sanitation." Every society has its misfits, and every society attempts to cope with and control this swirling, frequently troublesome, stream of human debris. In our society, our method of coping with troublesome misfits is incarceration, either in the mental hospital or in the prison.

Thus, marginal persons who become negatively visible to society at large by engaging in behaviors which violate the propriety norms (see Sarbin, 1967) are requested to live in these catchment areas. Those misfits who choose the institutional life initiate negative visibility (for example, they purposely act "crazy" in public), and in this way assure to some extent the kind of institution to which they will retreat (in this example, a mental hospital). Others become negatively visible because of a variety of contingencies, and the kind of institution in which they will reside is chosen for them. In both instances the incarceration is primarily a function of society's wish to keep its house in order rather than the result of any *defects* of the mind. These points will be elaborated further in Chapter 7.

The defect-free, sociopsychological conception of institutionalized adults that we evolved led us to the question to which we presently address our efforts: What happens to the children of the unsettled, marginal, disreputable poor? Surely, social misfits beget children: How, then, does society treat the children of these misfits?

Our experience with the dominant psychiatric conception of "mentally ill" adults led us to expect that the essential nature of the social problems confronting marginal children similarly would be misconstrued, being placed into the obscuring context of a medical or defect model. Specifically, the marginality, negative visibility, and institutionalization of the adult misfit has been explained away conveniently by psychiatry, which attributes their occurrence to some defective process of the mind rather than to the outcome of certain social and political forces. We expected, therefore, that the children of misfits who violate the mainstream norms would be managed and handled in the same manner. That is, the children's marginality, negative visibility, and institutionalization also would be explained away by some defect of the mind—particularly, familial mental retardation.

For this reason we expected to find a large number—perhaps a majority—of children residing in institutions for the retarded incarcerated not because they were intrinsically defective but instead because they had been caught up in the machinery of social sanitation. Just as we found rootless and rejected rather than defective adults in institutions for the insane, so did we anticipate finding rootless and rejected, rather than defective, children in institutions for the retarded.

Here we are making two distinctions concerning the institutionalization of children: first, there is the actual phenomenon that leads to the incarceration of children; and second, there is the societal and professional conception of why children must be incarcerated. The refrain of the professional is that children are institutionalized because they are mentally retarded. By using the concept of mental retardation the actual phenomenon involved in the institutionalization of children is obscured and the "true" nature of such children is obfuscated. We believe that the process of social sanitation and our assumption of the "normality" of these children leads to a better fit with reality than the pseudo-explanations proffered by the experts. The reader, of course, will be in a position to determine for himself, after examining our empirical findings, the validity of our model.

THE VALUES OF A NEW PARADIGM

The purpose of this chapter has been twofold: to demonstrate the inadequacy of the existing paradigms, and to present an alternate paradigm to mental retardation. Admittedly, the presentation of our approach has been sketchy, and it is only in the later chapters that the paradigm will take on detailed form. In addition, a number of reasons favoring the kind of paradigmatic shift we advocate have not always been stated explicitly. Although we have done so in our previous work with the mentally ill (Braginsky and others, 1969), and though the reasons here are identical, they are important enough to be reiterated.

The first reason is based upon the principle of parsimony. The dominant perspective of mental retardation requires that a special set of assumptions and concepts be applied to persons it designates as retarded. Apparently the principles governing the behavior of the rest of humanity are either not relevant or are insufficient where retardates are concerned. The paradigm we propose obviates the need for more than one set of principles and seeks to understand the behavior of all persons in terms of a common body of propositions.

The second reason for, and an obvious advantage of, the new paradigm is a heuristic one. A new conception of mental retardation will certainly not deprive us of any sound and hard-won knowledge; instead, it may awaken us to completely new and hitherto unthought-of possibilities, setting the stage for creative theoretical and research innovations.

The explanatory power of the new paradigm is another distinct advantage. As we have already suggested, the dominant conception of retardation obfuscates many aspects of the behavior of retardates by providing pseudo-answers to misconstrued questions. In the chapters that follow the data presented will provide the basis for an even more serious indictment of the traditional and dominant perspective.

Finally, the values one holds about men and their behavior forcibly enters into one's very conception of mental retardation. Accordingly, we should like, at this point, to express an explicit value judgment: in our opinion the traditional conception of retardation not only has impeded our scientific understanding but also has resulted in the dehumanization, degradation, and mismanagement of "mental retardates." The consequence of even such an innocuous aspect of the medical approach as diagnostic classification can be far-reaching as well as unjust, leading to possibly unintended yet potent psychic brutality. The new paradigm at least holds out the hope that, however one chooses to treat the "retardate," he will not be deprived of his essential humanity.

Characteristics of the Institutions and the Children

The research that will be presented in the next four chapters was conducted primarily at two large state institutions for the mentally retarded. In order to simplify our later presentation, as well as to enable the reader to understand the settings in which we worked, the state training schools and the residents we selected as subjects are described below.

THE INSTITUTIONS

The two training schools in which we conducted our research were similar in several respects. First, they were large, having a resident population of well over 1000. The residents included not only mental retardates but physically disabled persons as well. Second, they were geographically close, situated in bordering New England states. And, perhaps most important, they shared similar problems in resident management, staffing, funding, and public relations. Compared to most state institutions, both training schools were "good," providing relatively favorable settings for the residents.

There were, however, some striking differences between the two institutions. One training school, which we will call M, had comparatively modern buildings and facilities, while the other training school, F, spoke of a bygone era. In addition, training school M had a close, productive relationship with a nearby university, whereas the integration of training school F with institutions of higher learning was more limited. In general, training school M was more self-conscious of its operations, and more restrictive and formal in the management of its residents than training school F.

THE SUBJECTS

The residents of the training schools who were selected to serve as subjects had to meet the following criteria: (a) educable; (b) probably cultural-familial retardates—that is, they did not have any obvious organic impairment accounting for their low IQ scores; (c) judged by the training school staff to be capable of a relatively high degree of self-management. These criteria were met by approximately 40 percent of the residents. From this group we selected 177 subjects, divided almost equally between the sexes (one less girl). One hundred of the subjects were from training school F and 77 matched subjects came from training school M.

Table 1 presents a summary of the IQ range of the 177 subjects. As one can see, our selection criteria for subjects affected the IQ distribution of our sample: there were no profoundly retarded subjects, and only 2 percent had IQ scores of less than 35 (*severe* retardation). Thirty-four percent were *moderately* retarded with IQ scores between 36 and 51; 44 percent had IQ scores between 52 and 67, *mild* retardation; and 20 percent

TABLE 1

The Distribution of Levels
of Retardation for 177 Subjects

LEVEL	IQ RANGE	PERCENTAGE OF SAMPLE
1. Borderline	68–83	20
2. Mild	52–67	44
3. Moderate	36–51	34
4. Severe	20–35	2
5. Profound	19 & under	0

were considered *borderline* retardates, having IQ scores between 68 and 83.

In Table 2 the average age, length of time in the training school, percentage of life spent in the institution, and diagnostic level of the 177 subjects are presented by institution. All of

TABLE 2

Means and Standard Deviations
for 177 Subjects
on Four Demographic Variables

	INSTITUTION F $N = 100$		INSTITUTION M $N = 77$	
	MEAN	SD	MEAN	SD
1. Age	20.21	6.14	20.38	6.39
2. Length of hospitalization	10.05	5.59	9.43	5.85
3. Percent of life in institution	47.73	18.23	44.18	19.12
4. Diagnostic level	2.16	.77	2.03	.58

our subjects were between the ages of twelve and thirty. The average, or "typical," subject was in his late teens or early twenties, had spent about ten years in the training school (about half of his life), and was considered mildly retarded (IQ scores between 52 and 67).

All of the 177 subjects were used in our largest study, where they were administered questionnaires and interviewed extensively. Some of our experimental studies, however, employed smaller samples. In addition, our research took us to other settings including a public high school and a small private institution for the retarded. These smaller samples and the different settings will be described along with the studies in which they were involved in the later chapters.

CHAPTER

3

Children in Institutions:
Studies of Their Effectiveness
in Interpersonal Manipulation

Power, in a variety of forms, has been the goal of many men. Man's perseverance in his search for it, the tenacity with which he maintains and guards it, and how he uses and abuses power have been amply documented throughout recorded history. Power has been and still is a commodity that appeals to almost everyone—the strong as well as the weak, the rich as well as the poor, the young as well as the old. It is a rare commodity—made rare by a number of complex personal and cultural contrivances. It is, in fact, so rare that each culture carefully "rations" it, selectively doling it out in varying amounts to its members. In this culture selective "rationing" of power can be seen clearly when we examine how children and adults are allocated this commodity.

Children, more than adults, suffer from a severe power disadvantage. Our culture does not allocate power in any appreciable amounts to the young. To be a child means that adults have the right to control the most trifling details of one's life. A child, then, is a person whose power has been formally preempted by adults. There is, however, another group who occupies a power position lower still than that of the normal child—the children in institutions for the retarded. The child diagnosed as retarded has had his power preempted by adults not merely because of his age, but more importantly because of his assumed defect. While the normal child in our culture is implicitly seen and treated as a "defective adult" (albeit a transient one), the retarded youngster is viewed and usually handled as a "defective child." The consequences of this perception of the retardate are numerous and profound; one of them is the zero formal power status of the retarded child.

As any parent can tell us, our discussion of child power cannot be complete if it ignores the counterpower strategies employed by children. For the most part, "normal" children do not blindly acquiesce to the demands of parents, teachers, and other significant adults. Children are, indeed, notorious for their single-minded pursuit of goals even in the face of contradictory demands made by the adult world. Children do attempt to control their own fates, and if faced with an imposed, undesirable one, they will attempt to resist it or, that failing, escape it.

If the child's efforts to counteract the power of adults are successful, then the adult's control over the child is not as all-encompassing and effective as it appears at first. That is, the formal and legitimate power of the adult can be mitigated to a considerable extent by the application of counterpower by the child. And this happens frequently. It is important, however, to distinguish between the nature of the power children and adults can exploit. The power of the adult or parent is *legitimate power*, ordained to them by society and sanctioned by law and custom. The power that children can employ, however, is *subversive* in nature—power that is achieved primarily by undermining and violating the adult power system in subtle and usually disguised ways. The "balance of power" between adult and child thus is a balance between the formal, sanctioned power of the adult and the covert, illegitimate power of the child.

IMPRESSION MANAGEMENT AS A FORM OF CHILD COUNTERPOWER

A child can "borrow" some adult power through a multitude of manipulative strategies. One such strategy is what Goffman (1959) has termed "impression management." By this term Goffman means that in interpersonal situations we manage our expressive behavior so as to control the impressions others form of us. It is a strategy that makes it possible for the child, business executive, salesman, politician, college professor, and parent to perform their roles in society successfully. Impression management permeates behavior at dinner tables, cocktail parties, job interviews, conventions, and seminars. In short, it is a manipulative strategy that many people use, and which occurs in all sorts of social situations. The pervasiveness of impression management and the youthfulness of some of the impression managers, however, does not belie either simplicity in its acquisition nor ease in its implementation. To the contrary, impression management is an extremely demanding interpersonal skill. In order to appreciate just how demanding it is, let us briefly examine some of the abilities it requires.

To be manipulative first requires that one has a manipulative orientation. The impression manager first must be interested in having some control over his relations with others. If he wants to be successful at exerting even a modicum of control, he must develop a rather extensive and articulated body of information about human behavior. There must be recognition of the necessity and importance of defining and steering social situations; the kinds and effectiveness of power and counterpower strategies available to him; the importance of selectively disclosing and censoring information about one's self; the use of verbal and nonverbal forms of communication in shaping the responses of others, and so on.

Moreover, the impression manager must learn how to act under conditions more difficult than those met by the professional actor. Specifically, the impression manager has to be able to extract, receive, discriminate, evaluate, and weigh large amounts of information about his "audience." He then must develop rapidly an effective "script" which he can use to shape and control the impressions his audience forms of him. Along with the development of his script is the requirement to perform it as well. That is, he must translate the script into a concrete, believable performance. While engaged in the performance, the impression manager must monitor his audience in order to determine how well he is doing, so that he may make any adjustments in the script necessary to realign his behavior with audience expectations. Perhaps most crucial and most ironic, he must be able to convince his audience that he is, in fact, not an "actor."

A cursory analysis of the strategy of impression management, then, makes it clear that it is not "child's play," but hard work. It requires complex knowledge, discipline, creativity, and a great deal of social and emotional awareness. Because of its demands, people given a choice will avoid using it. There are some conditions, however, which facilitate the appearance of this strategy (see especially Jones, 1964).

CONDITIONS NECESSARY FOR THE AROUSAL OF IMPRESSION MANAGEMENT

Let us suppose that Jim, a very poor student who never studies, is promised a new bike by his parents if he studies every day for an entire month. Every afternoon Jim closes himself in his room to daydream, listen to the ball game, and so on. When he hears his parents' footsteps approach his door, however, he buries his nose in a book, furrows his brow in deep thought, and occupies himself with his notes. He hopes to make a "good impression" on his folks so that at the end of the thirty days his new bike will materialize.

Let us also suppose that John wants very much to get a position as a bank teller. He goes for an interview knowing that he must make a particular kind of impression (he must be seen as a clean-cut, honest, reliable man). He meets the interviewer and communicates through verbal (what he says) and nonverbal (for example, how he looks) means his honesty, morality, pleasantness, and so on, hoping that he will foster the right impression and get the job.

These two examples have much in common. Both actors have intense needs or goals; both are very much dependent upon someone else for the realization of their goals; and in both situations the other person has expectations as to how the actors should behave. We can state these three factors in the following formula: The probability of impression management $= f$ (the intensity of actor's needs $\times$ the degree of actor's dependency on others $\times$ the others' expectations about the actor's behavior). In our two examples all three factors have high values; thus the probability that Jim and John will engage in impression management in order to control the behavior of the parents and the interviewer is high. In short, when any person (P) has an important goal; is dependent upon others (O) for the realization of this goal; and O has clearly defined standards of conduct for P; then P will most likely engage in impression management. If any one of these factors is low, then the probability of P engaging in this manipulative strategy is also low.

What does this all have to do with retardation? The notion that normal children can employ impression management in the service of their own motivations is not surprising. Indeed, our notion that retarded children also engage in impression management, and are probably even more inclined to use it than others (because their objective situation makes them more dependent on others), might be a point hardly worth mentioning were it not for the prevailing view of retardation. Cognitively, socially and emotionally inferior organisms should not be capable of such sophisticated, complex, and abstract gestures. This kind of interaction certainly collides with the view of the retardate as being deficient in judgment and social adaptation.

From our standpoint, however, we expect that the retardate is not only capable of impression management, but also that he uses it surprisingly successfully (perhaps in part because of the expectations of others that he is incapable of dissembling at all). If one is ready to grant at the outset that the retardate is no different from most of us, the findings to be presented will come as no surprise. If, however, one is not accustomed to viewing retardates in this way, their experimentally induced behavior may occasion a shock of sorts.

THE "CULTURAL-FAMILIAL" MACHIAVELLIAN

As we have stated earlier, a necessary (but not sufficient) condition for impression management to occur at all is the presence of a manipulative orientation. Our first research efforts, therefore, are directed to the question of whether retardates have the ability to master an orientation typically assumed to be in the domain of the intelligent. Specifically, we ask the question whether retardates maintain Machiavellian attitudes and subscribe to Machiavellian tactics in interpersonal situations.

Christie (1962), on the basis of a content analysis of Machiavelli's work, developed an attitude scale (Mach Scale) that measures an individual's predisposition to employ manipulative tactics for self-seeking reasons. This scale has not only been successful in differentiating between people, but an impressive array of data supporting its ability to identify the successful manipulators has been compiled. In order, however, to assess these same Machiavellian attitudes in children, a new version of the Mach Scale suitable for children was developed by D. Braginsky (1966, 1970)—one which required little verbal sophistication. The children's Mach Scale which we employed in our study was composed of sixteen items, half of which were keyed in a *True* direction (meaning a response of true to the item obtained a Mach score) and half in a *False* direction. The sixteen items were embedded in both the retardate and staff attitude tests (described in Chapters 4 and 5). The attitude tests, including the Mach Scale, were individually administered to the retardates, and administered in groups to the staff. These Machiavellian scores were obtained for 177 retardates, 50 professional staff members, and 45 matrons and aides.

The mean Mach score for the retardates was 7.61, for the professional staff 5.00, and for the subprofessionals, 5.91. Analyses of these data show that retardates obtain significantly higher Mach scores than both the professionals ($t = 8.13$, $p < 001$), and the aides and matrons ($t = 4.25$, $p < 001$).

An examination of the responses to the items presented in Table 3 makes it evident that the retardates maintain more cynical, mistrustful, and manipulatively-oriented attitudes than either staff group. For example, 89 percent of the retardates (as compared to 12 percent of the professionals and 22 percent of the aides) agreed that "The best way to handle people is to tell them what they want to hear." Moreover, an overwhelming majority of the retardates compared to a small percent of the staff agree to these items: "Never tell anyone the real reason you did something unless it will be helpful to you." "It is hard to get ahead without cheating." "It's a smart thing to be nice to important people."

One possible reason for the retardates' higher Mach scores is that the staff may not disclose what they consider to be socially undesirable attitudes. We believe, however, that a more parsimonious and plausible reason for the difference is that retardates have much more to be cynical and manipulative about than does the institutional staff. Staff members in their dealings with retardates do not have to engage in the subtle artifice of manipulation to accomplish their goals; instead, they have the backing and power of the institution to give impetus to their declarations. Retardates, on the other hand, must resort to manipulation in order to control the responses of the staff. This, however, is not the important finding. What we wish to underline is that the retardates demonstrated that they are not only aware of Machiavellian strategies, but that they endorse them as well. We have unearthed, then, the cultural-familial Machiavellian—a "diagnostic" subtype which, as we will see soon, is necessary for survival in institutional settings.

TABLE 3

Machiavellian Attitudes of Retardates,
Aides, and Professional Staff

ITEM	PERCENTAGE AGREEMENT		
	PROF.	AIDES	RET.
1. It is better to be a person who is unimportant and honest than to be one who is important and dishonest.	98	96	69 *
2. The best way to handle people is to tell them what they want to hear.	12	22	89 *
3. A person can be good in every way.	24	39	84 *
4. Never tell anyone the real reason you did something unless it will be helpful to you.	4	25	70 **
5. Anyone who completely trusts anyone else is asking for trouble.	16	27	47 *
6. Most people won't work hard at things unless they are forced to.	26	33	67 *
7. People should be sure they are doing the right thing before they do it.	78	84	85 N.S.
8. The saying that there is a sucker (fool) born every minute is right.	30	54	71 **
9. Most people who get ahead in the world lead good clean lives.	30	37	86 *
10. Most men are brave.	40	43	88 *
11. You can be sure that most people have a mean streak and they will show it whenever they have the chance.	14	57	88 **

TABLE 3 (*continued*)

ITEM	PERCENTAGE AGREEMENT		
12. It's a smart thing to be nice to important people.	54	54	93 *
13. Honesty is always the best policy.	82	87	87 N.S.
14. Most people are good and kind.	68	74	92 *
15. There are good reasons for lying sometimes.	68	63	60 N.S.
16. It is hard to get ahead without cheating.	4	13	69 *
Mean Mach Scores	5.00	5.91	7.61
S.D.	2.25	2.58	1.80

* $p < .05$
** $p < .01$

THE BATTLE: RETARDATE GOALS AND INSTITUTIONAL DEMANDS

Although direct evidence will be presented in later chapters, for the time being we will assume that there is a covert, intense, bitter, and enduring conflict between the resident (retardates) and the staff in institutions for the retarded—a battle not unlike that found in mental hospitals between patients and staff. It is basically an ideological battle, in which the retardates' beliefs concerning who they are, what they are like, the reasons for their incarceration, the nature of their keepers, and so on are in direct opposition to those maintained by the institution and its representatives. This ideological chasm has a number of consequences for both parties. For the retardates it facilitates the development of a Machiavellian orientation and also shapes the kinds of impression management strategies that they will employ (if, of course, retardates are capable of employing manipulative strategies). The zero power status of the retardates, therefore, poses the interrelated problems of (1) implementing goals and life styles that may be institutionally devalued; (2) maintaining conceptions about themselves that may be discrepant with those held by the staff; and (3) accomplishing all of this without invoking the ire of the institution and its employees.

The retardates' lack of power is aggravated further by the "supreme" power granted to the institution by our society. For example, on the outside world, a child is beholden to only a few adults. Not all adults have the same power over the non-institutionalized child as his parents do. Thus, *outside* children have to concern themselves with only a very small number of relevant people. Retardates, the *inside* children, lack this econ-omy of effort. Instead, they must satisfy and contend with a multitude of adults, all of whom have the same degree of power over him as his parents would have if he were home. *Every* adult in the institution, from housekeeper to superintend-ent, has the power to control the retardate's life. The retard-ate, then, in order to safeguard his status (that is, to avoid criticism or punishment) must maintain "good" relationships with *all* the staff he encounters, even though he may not share their beliefs and goals, or even like them. This is a task that would no doubt overburden some very sophisticated and adept adults.

Under these conditions, interpersonal "squalls" can be dan-gerous and painful for the retardate. We would expect that when the retardate encounters his superiors he will act in a way that will "not rock the boat." This would imply, for ex-ample, that retardates would be reluctant to criticize openly institution policies or staff, or express beliefs that run counter to those expected by the institution. One form of their impres-sion management can, accordingly, be anticipated to reflect this primary motivation.

IMPRESSION MANAGEMENT
THROUGH INGRATIATION

Jones (1964) has suggested that *ingratiation* may be regarded as an illicit interpersonal tactic that can be used to secure bene-

its (or to avoid harm) from others. He maintains that ingratiation is illicit because it takes place within a normative frame-
work that it appears to honor but in fact does not. Ingratiation,
according to Jones, involves an attempt to increase one's attrac-
tiveness to others who have the power to reward or punish the
individual; in this way, the ingratiator, if he is successful, can
increase the likelihood of achieving good outcomes (or avoid-
ing bad ones). Ingratiation may take many forms: one may
flatter the target person, agree with his opinions, present oneself in an engagingly modest way, and so on.

As we noted earlier in this chapter, the conditions that are
very often present within the institution facilitate the use of
impression management. Our analysis of the retardate's power
position suggested both his dependence on others and his
likely recourse to illegitimate forms of power (of which ingratiation is an obvious example) to achieve his goals. Furthermore, because ingratiation involves presenting oneself in such
a way as to influence the impressions others form of him, it
clearly represents one instance of behavior in the service of
impression management. All these considerations point to an
empirically verifiable assertion: retardates can be expected to
manage their impressions, through the use of ingratiation
tactics, in their interactions with the staff. The following study,
by providing retardates with the opportunity to engage in
ingratiation through flattery, permits a test of this hypothesis.

For this study a thirty-item test labeled "Opinions About the
Training School" was constructed. This test was based on an
earlier "Opinion Inventory" (Braginsky, Braginsky, and Ring,
1969) used to assess ingratiation with institutionalized mental
patients. The items, to be answered true or false, were of three
types: (1) eleven items that expressed highly implausible but
positive opinions about the institution (for example, "There is
nothing about the training school that needs improvement of
any kind"; "Every single matron and attendant in this school is
as good to us as a mother and father would be to their child");
(2) nine realistic but mildly critical opinions about the training
school (for example, "There are times when I feel that some
of the staff do not quite understand me"; "There are times
when I wish the training school treated me better"); and (3)

ten unrealistically critical opinions about the training school ("The training school always takes advantage of the retardates"; "There is not a single good thing about being a retardate in this school"). Since we investigated the use of ingratiation in other institutions as well (a private school for the retarded and a public high school), slight modifications were made in order to make the test appropriate to these different settings. Copies of these forms can be found in Appendix B.

It seems reasonable, in view of the content of these items, to assume that retardates who tend to agree with the first type and disagree with the second type are expressing exaggeratedly and unrealistically positive opinions about their institutions. No institution with which we are familiar comes close to meriting this praise. Whether such hyperbole can be taken as indicative of ingratiation or some other factor(s) mainly depends on the nature of the test-taking instructions which are considered next.

Two experimental conditions, which differed in the instructions Ss received concerning the test, were created. In the *Public* condition, Ss were told:

> We are here today to find out how you feel about this school. That is, we are interested in your opinions. On this questionnaire, you will find statements which measure how you feel about this school and its staff. We would like you to answer them as accurately as possible. *Please sign your name* on the top of both pages. This is very important because some of the training school staff will review these tests later and they would like to know which people filled out which tests. That is, they will want to identify who took the tests. This can only be done if you sign your name. Thank you.

In the *Anonymous* condition, Ss received this induction:

> We are here to find out how you feel about the training school. That is, we are interested in your opinions. On this questionnaire, you will find statements which measure how you feel about this school and its staff. We would like you to answer them as ac-

curately as possible. *Please do not sign your name* to the tests. We are not interested in who takes the test. All we are interested in is how you, as a group, feel about the school. So remember, do not sign your name. Thank you.

It will be obvious that of the two conditions, Ss in the *Public* condition ought to be more highly instigated to ingratiate themselves, if our assumptions about their motivations are sound. Only they as individuals have something to lose through endorsement of opinions critical of the institution; only they as individuals stand to gain by praising the institution and its staff. Ss in this condition, therefore, have a twofold motivation to ingratiate themselves: to avoid arousing the censure of the staff (prompting disagreement with the critical items) and to increase the likelihood of continued favorable treatment (prompting agreement with the positive items). Because they individually can receive neither credit for the approved response nor blame for disapproved ones, Ss in the *Anonymous* condition should show considerably less evidence of a desire to ingratiate themselves.

The first sample tested were residents of a large state institution. The sample consisted of 20 children (13 boys and 7 girls). The mean length of institutionalization was 3.8 years, with a standard deviation of 3.3 years. The mean age of the subjects was 14.5 years, with a standard deviation of 2.4 years. The mean mental age of the sample was 7.5 years, with a standard deviation of 1.4 years. Each experimental group was composed of 10 subjects (7 boys and 3 girls in one group, 6 boys and 4 girls in the other). A comparison of these variables between experimental conditions failed to disclose any significant differences. The tests were group administered. In order to insure that the Ss understood the items, the examiner read out loud each item, making sure that all Ss completed the item (by a show of hands) before progressing to the next one.

Table 4 presents the mean number of items answered in an ingratiating direction. It is clear that, as expected, Ss in the *Public* condition responded to the test items in an ingratiating fashion significantly more often than the *Anonymous* group

TABLE 4

*Mean Number of Ingratiating Test Responses
for Retardates in Institution M*

PUBLIC CONDITION	ANONYMOUS CONDITION
10.60	6.30
($N = 10$)	($N = 10$)

($p < .01$). No significant relationships were found between the demographic variables (mental age, and so on) and test responses.

Ten unrealistically critical items had been incorporated into the test in order to evaluate the possibility that low ingratiation scores reflected not simply realistically critical appraisals of the institution but instead obviously unwarranted, negativistic ones. Because we found a low absolute incidence of endorsement of such items in both conditions (means of 1.25 and 1.98 for the *Public* and *Anonymous* conditions, respectively), this interpretation is effectively ruled out. Low ingratiation scores are not indicative of hypercritical attitudes about the institution.

In order to see whether these findings could be replicated in another institution, we conducted a second study. The sample was composed of 27 children (12 males and 15 females) living in a small private school for the retarded. Although this was a private school, most of the subjects were financially supported by the State. This group had a mean age of 14.8 years, with a standard deviation of 2.9. The mean mental age of the subjects was 7.8 years, with a standard deviation of 2.4. The mean length of institutionalization was 7.6 years. There were no significant differences between experimental groups on the demographic characteristics. Both sexes were represented equally in the experimental conditions.

Table 5 presents the mean number of items answered in an ingratiating direction. Again, as expected, Ss in the *Public* condition achieved significantly higher ingratiation scores

TABLE 5

*Mean Number of Ingratiating Test Responses
for Retardates in Institution S*

PUBLIC CONDITION	ANONYMOUS CONDITION
10.20	7.75
($N = 15$)	($N = 12$)

(p. $< .01$). These scores, in fact, were almost identical to those obtained in our first study.

Our predictions, which were supported by these data, were based on a model that makes no recourse to "defects" of any kind; instead, it is a model based on assumptions of normality. The "retardates," then, behaved in the same manner we would expect a normal high-school or college student to, given structurally similar conditions. In order to leave little room for doubt about this position, we conducted a third study using as subjects normal public high-school students. High-school students, obviously, do not occupy the same life conditions as residents in an institution for the retarded. For one thing, they are not extremely dependent on the institution, and they have more than zero power in their fate determination. Referring back to our formula of the probability of impression management occurring, we can assume that the value for the dependency factor would be significantly lower for a student in high school than for a retardate in an institution. This being true, we would expect less absolute ingratiation occurring in high school than in institutions for the retarded. In terms of the relative distribution of ingratiation, we should find, nonetheless, more ingratiation in a *Public* condition, where the high-school student can be held accountable for his views about his school and teachers, than in an *Anonymous* situation. With this in mind, 78 high school subjects were tested in the same manner as the retardates, but with a modified Opinion Inventory and an induction more appropriate to the high school. The mean age of the population was 15.7 years, with a standard deviation of .79.

The Ss were students in two randomly selected study halls (the entire study halls participated). The experimenter was introduced by the proctor as a person interested in conducting an opinion poll.

The induction for the *Public condition* for high school students was as follows:

> We are here today to find out how you feel about the school. That is, we are interested in your opinions. On this questionnaire you will find statements which measure how you feel about this school and your teachers. We would like you to answer them as accurately as possible. *Please sign your name* on the top of both pages and fill in your home room number. This is very important because after you complete the questionnaire, your principal, your teachers, and your guidance counselor will review them and they will want to know which students filled out which tests. This can only be done if you sign your name clearly and fill in your room number. Thank you.

In the *Anonymous condition* subjects were given this induction:

> We are here today to find out how you feel about the school. That is, we are interested in your opinions. On this questionnaire you will find statements which measure how you feel about this school and your teachers. We would like you to answer them as accurately as possible. *Please do not sign your name* at the top of the page and do not fill in your home room number. We are not interested in who takes the test. All we are interested in is how you students, as a group, feel about the school. So remember, please do not sign your name. Thank you.

The results in Table 6 again indicate a significant difference between ingratiation scores in the two experimental conditions (p. $<.025$). High-school students, like "retardates," are more flattering about the institution and its staff when they can be held accountable for their opinions. The high-school students, as we expected, were in general less ingratiating than the retardates.

It seems only reasonable to conclude that the data from the present series of studies are consistent with the ingratiation

TABLE 6

*Mean Number of Ingratiating Test Responses
for Public High School Students*

PUBLIC CONDITION	ANONYMOUS CONDITION
4.38	2.87
($N = 40$)	($N = 38$)

hypotheses and with the assumptions that retardates can engage in impression management. The data suggest that retardates are quite capable of acting in their own self-interests, at least to the extent of misrepresenting their own opinions about the "goodness" of the institution and its staff. Thus, the retardates have available and use an efficient and effective strategy for "not rocking the boat." Imagine—retardates, like most normals, show good "common" sense!

Don't rock boat — Ret. Show good Common Sense!

Safeguarding one's status is only a portion of what the retardate must accomplish in his confrontation with the institution. In addition he must be alert to the decisions made about him by the staff, and when these decisions are contrary to his goals he must attempt to subvert them. For example, a number of institutional decisions concerning retardates are based upon the staffs' conception of how "bright" the retardate is. Thus, if a decision about who attends school classes must be made, usually those retardates who are considered "educable" are sent. Sometimes staff decisions correspond to the personal needs and goals of the retardate—he may wish to go to the institution's school. More often than not, we expect staff decisions to be discrepant with retardate goals. The question this raises is: Will retardates actively attempt to control and, if need be, subvert staff decisions, or do they passively acquiesce to whatever fate is in store for them?

The retardates themselves explicitly answer this question. In our interviews with 177 retardates, 95 percent of them say that they are *not* retarded. Moreover, 86 percent of this group report that they will not show the institutional staff just how bright they really are. The reasons they offer are numerous (for example, not wishing to get the staff angry; not wanting certain jobs in the institution; wanting to remain in the institution). Most of the reasons deal directly with their desire for some degree of fate determination. That is, their goal is to undermine the efficacy of staff decisions while increasing their own. So, for instance, to the question: "Are there some people here who are considered retarded but who are brighter than some of the institution's staff?", 90 percent of the subjects responded in the affirmative. But when asked: "Do these people show the staff that they are brighter?", 86 percent of the retardates said no.

Again, the reasons they offered reflect their desire to increase their power in fate determination while weakening the staff's. From the point of view of the retardates, they are not passive in their confrontations with the institution. But can we believe them?

THE "NOW BRIGHT" AND "THEN DUMB" RETARDATE VERSUS THE "NOW DUMB" AND "THEN BRIGHT" RETARDATE

In order to test the validity of the retardates' and our assertions, we placed retardates in an experimental situation (although they experienced it as a real life event) that afforded them the opportunity to influence their fate by impression managing their IQ scores. Specifically, we gave them the opportunity to misrepresent their IQ's in order to "cop out" of a hypothetical educational program we thought they would find undesirable.

The subjects for this study were told by the building attendants to report to a room for testing. Once in the testing room each S was administered individually the Full Range Picture Vocabulary Test (Ammons & Ammons, 1948), an IQ test. This test is very highly related to other standard tests of intelligence, such as the WISC. The FRPV had three distinct advantages for our study: first, it could be given in a relatively short period of time; second, verbal responses were not required of the Ss, but instead they had to point to the pictures that best defined the words read aloud by the examiner; and, finally, there were two parallel forms of the test. Half of the Ss tested were given Form A and the others Form B.

Ten days later the Ss again reported to the testing room, where they were assigned randomly to one of three experimental conditions: High IQ, Low IQ, and Control. Prior to taking the IQ test again the Ss in both the High and Low IQ conditions were told:

A few days ago you were given an intelligence test, but we found that we used the wrong answer sheets and forms. So it will take only a few minutes to give you another IQ test. Then we can begin to select students for a new program we are planning. The staff here at the training school is thinking about starting a new intensive treatment program for a small group of students. The way that we see it now is that there will be 30 students living together on one unit with ten attendants for six months. This unit will not be in this building. From Monday through Saturday everyone will get up at six in the morning, go to school for 8 hours and be strictly supervised by a staff member. Every evening there will be special discussion groups with the attendants; then there will be one hour of an educational TV program selected by the staff. The lights are out at 7:30. Students will not be allowed to leave the building unless they are with an attendant; and there will be special TV cameras set up in every room so that the staff can always watch the students' behavior to see if they have any bad habits that need to be corrected.

In the *High* IQ condition the following was added:

FOR THIS PROGRAM, THE STAFF WILL SELECT ONLY THOSE STUDENTS WHO HAVE HIGH IQ SCORES BECAUSE THEY THINK THE SMART STUDENTS WOULD BENEFIT MOST FROM THIS PROGRAM.

In the *Low* IQ test condition the Ss were told:

FOR THIS PROGRAM, THE STAFF WILL SELECT ONLY THOSE STUDENTS

WHO HAVE LOW IQ SCORES BECAUSE THEY THINK THE SLOW STU-
DENTS NEED THIS TREATMENT THE MOST.

The *Control* condition was identical to the initial testing procedure, having only the standard directions for the test administration. All Ss who were given Form A initially were now
administered Form B; those who took Form B the first time
were given Form A. The examiners did not know the Ss' initial
IQ scores since they were not scored until the experiment was
completed. The 36 subjects were all boys; their mean age was
16.4 years (SD = 2.8); their mean mental age was 9.9 years
(SD = 1.9); and their mean length of institutionalization was
5.2 years (SD = 1.2). The subjects were selected randomly
from all the retardates in one building (over the age of 12
years). Not all of the subjects showed up at the appointed time
for re-testing, leaving us with unequal numbers in each of the
conditions. Since those Ss who participated were told the purpose of the experiment after their testing, we could not re-
schedule those subjects who were not available nor select new
subjects.

If we inspect the mental age scores in Table 7, we find that
there are no significant differences between the means for the
three experimental conditions nor between the first and second
test mean scores. Thus, it would appear that our inductions had
no effect whatsoever on the subjects' test performance. Despite
the fact that the group means did not change, rather large
individual changes in mental age (MA) between test 1 and
test 2 were observed for many of the Ss both in the High and
Low conditions, while no individual shifts in mental age were
found for the control Ss. The control group test-retest data, in
fact, replicates the relationships reported by Ammons and Ammons (1962) for their standardization group. The correlation
between both tests for our control group was .93 ($p < .001$),
and for the standardization group, .99. This indicates that the
FRPV test is indeed a reliable measure of "intelligence" (at
least, over a short period of time).

On the other hand, the correlation between the two tests
for our High and Low IQ conditions was .35 (not significant),
indicating a failure to replicate the first test score after the

verbal induction was given. The difference between the correlations obtained for the control group and the experimental group is, of course, significant ($z = 3.05$, $p < .01$).

What this means, then, is that there was a great deal of change induced (though not in the predicted directions) by our hypothetical "training program." If we inspect only the magnitude of change, disregarding whether it is higher or lower on test 2, the experimental groups ($\overline{X} = 1.96$ years) shifted significantly more than the control group ($\overline{X} = .80$ years; $F = 4.76$, $p = .03$). Thus, 34 percent of the experimental Ss showed a change of more than two years of mental age (for example, going from a MA of 8 to 10), while not one of the control subjects changed nearly as much.

TABLE 7

Mean Mental Age Scores under Standard and Experimental Induction Conditions

	FIRST TEST	SECOND TEST
High IQ Induction ($N = 13$)	9.74	9.96
Low IQ Induction ($N = 13$)	10.16	10.61
Control ($N = 10$)	9.99	9.29

It seems quite plausible then, to conclude that chance factors were not operating and that the inductions did influence the retardates' behavior. What is most obvious is that not all of the subjects perceived our induction negatively, as we thought they would. Some subjects changed scores in a manner that would make them maximally eligible for our hypothetical program. In the Low IQ condition, five of the eleven subjects responded with a lower mental age on the second test than would have been predicted on the basis of their first tests. In the High IQ condition, four of the ten subjects increased their second test scores, thereby appearing significantly brighter than one would have guessed on the basis of their first test. To our surprise, these subjects performed in a manner that would facilitate entry into the hypothetical program. Why would these youngsters want to be in such a restrictive, unenjoyable, downright unpleasant program?

A reexamination of our induction led to an interesting possibility: perhaps these nine youngsters were not interested in *getting into* our highly restrictive hypothetical "program," but rather were motivated to *get out* of the building they were in now. Entry into our suggested program would afford them this opportunity. We were further puzzled, since the building these subjects lived in was the most modern and comfortable one in the institution. Thus we were led to conclude that the desire of wanting "out" had to emanate from poor social relationships within their present dwelling. That is, these nine subjects might be the building "scapegoats"—they might have unpleasant relationships with the staff and/or other residents in the building.

We set out to test this admittedly belated insight by describing the hypothetical program and giving a list of all our subjects to the aide in charge of the building, asking him to rate each S (experimental and control) on the following dimensions:

(1) How much is (name of S) liked by the other kids in the building?

(2) How much is (name of S) liked by the staff in the building?

(3) How much do you think (name of S) would like to leave this building?

(4) How often does (name of S) get into trouble here?

(5) How interested do you think (name of S) would be in getting into the program (which is described to the charge aide)?

The items were rated on a five-point scale ranging from Very Much (5) to None At All (1). The results are presented in Table 8. An analysis of variance of the data demonstrated that the subjects who *maximized* their chances of entry into the program as compared to those who *minimized* their chances, were rated as less liked by the other "kids" in the building (F

= 13.64; $p < .01$); less liked by the staff in the building ($F = 45.70$; $p < .001$); and probably more interested in getting into our hypothetical program ($F = 7.63$; $p < .02$). There were no differences between the two groups on questions 3 and 4.

TABLE 8

Aide's Ratings of Maximizers and Minimizers

	MINIMIZERS	MAXIMIZERS
1. How much S is liked by other kids in building.	4.1	3.1**
2. How much S is liked by the staff in building.	4.5	3.1***
3. How much charge-aide thinks S would like to leave the building.	3.4	4.1
4. How often S gets into trouble.	1.9	2.3
5. How interested charge-aide thinks S would like to be in hypothetical program.	2.8	4.2*

* $p < .025$ ** $p < .01$ *** $p < .001$

The subjects who tried to maximize their chances of getting out of their building were not different from the other Ss on any other variables (for example, mental age, length of institutionalization, age). Although these findings are not conclusive evidence for motivations underlying IQ test performance, they are highly suggestive. Obviously, other plausible motivations could be offered. The important point, however, is that significant and large changes in mental age occurred under our inductions, and these changes were related significantly to the charge aide's perception of the subjects. Although we might not have clearly explicated the motives underlying the test performances, we have demonstrated that retardates, if they want to, can manage their impressions through intelligence test scores.

In the next study, therefore, we attempted to establish a more precise relationship between motives and test performance. The subjects in this study were recruited from a private school for the mentally retarded; this school offered an excellent physical and social environment for children. It was selected precisely for this reason, for it provided a backdrop against which our experimental induction could be very potent. That is, the induction threatened their stay at this school, and since our subjects were supported by the state, it was clearly in their self-interests to remain there.

The subjects were assembled in a large room and were informed that they were all going to receive an intelligence test. Subjects were then drawn individually from the room and were administered the Quick Test (see Ammons and Ammons, 1962), a short picture vocabulary test having three different forms. All subjects were given Form I followed by Form II; the two forms correlate .98 with each other. The experimenter, after introducing himself, told the subject:

> I'm going to show you some pictures and say some words. When I say a word, show me which of the pictures best fits it. Some of the words are going to be rather hard. Just say you "don't know." (After the subject completes the FIRST TEST) That was fine, but it was only a practice test. I'm going to throw this one away and give you another one very similar to the test you just took. (EXPERIMENTER CRUMPLES TEST AND TOSSES IT IN WASTEBASKET) Before we start the real test I think I should tell you why we are testing you. The State is thinking about starting a new training program for mentally retarded youngsters. I can't tell you the details about the new program, but from what I've heard I really don't think that you would like it. To me it sounded really terrible. Well, they want us to test a group of kids to see if they should be put in this new training program. You see, they only want to take
>
> Condition I.   kids who do well on this test—who get good IQ scores.
> Condition II.   kids who do poorly on this test—who get really low IQ scores.

Okay, now that you know why I'm testing you, let's begin the *real* IQ test. What's your name? (EXPERIMENTER WRITES SUBJECT'S NAME IN OBVIOUS WAY) You have to do the same thing as before, only now there will be different words and different pictures.

In the *Control Condition* the subjects were instructed:

That was fine, but it was only a practice test. I'm going to throw this one away and give you another one very similar to the test you just took. Okay. What's your name?

Upon completion of the task, the subjects were told the purpose of the experiment and were escorted out of the building. There was no communication, therefore, with waiting subjects.

Thirty subjects (23 boys and 7 girls) were equally distributed in each of the three conditions. There were no significant differences between conditions on demographic variables. The mean age of the subjects was 14.1 with a standard deviation of 2.5. The average time spent in an institution was 4.0 years. The mean mental age was 9.92 with a standard deviation of 2.3.

As in the previous study, we expected that the subjects would manipulate their IQ scores in order to satisfy their motives—in this case, to stay in the pleasant milieu of the school and/or to avoid being placed in a negative one. In order to achieve this goal, subjects in Condition I should appear less intelligent (get lower MA scores) in their second test; subjects in Condition II should attain higher MA scores (that is, appear brighter), while there should be no change for subjects in the control condition. Aside from significant differences between the subjects' first and second test scores, we anticipated also that the groups would differ with respect to the direction and magnitude of change.

Table 9 presents the mean MA scores obtained by each group on their first and second tests. Obviously, the control group showed almost no change, attesting to the high reliability of the two forms of the test. The subjects in Condition I, as predicted, decreased significantly in mental age on the second test ($t = 3.23$, $p < .01$); subjects in Condition II, again as

TABLE 9

*Mean Mental Age Scores on First
and Second Tests*

	FIRST TEST[*]	SECOND TEST	CHANGE
Condition I (N = 10)	10.50	8.95	−1.55
Condition II (N = 10)	9.40	11.75	+2.35
Control (N = 10)	9.85	9.90	+ .05

[*] There are no significant differences between the groups on first test.

anticipated, achieved significantly higher mental ages on test two ($t = 2.37, p < .025$).

In addition, comparisons between the three groups (analysis of variance) supported our prediction. As we can see in Table 9, the mean change in mental age for Condition I dropped over one and one-half years; whereas for Condition II the mental age was elevated more than two years, with no change in the control group. The differences between these groups were significant ($F = 6.51, p < .005$).

In this chapter we have presented the position that because of the extreme imbalance in power, and the differences in goals and concepts between the retardate and institution, retardates can be expected to develop and use counter-power tactics. These expectations were predicated on our beliefs about the nature of the "retardate" that we presented in Chapter 1. Simply stated here, retardates like everyone else have the ability to master the complex art of impression management and can use it effectively to control their fate in the institution. Retardates follow the same laws of human behavior as "normals," and their behavior can be understood and predicted using the same terms and models we employ to understand "normal" behavior.

The data presented in our studies make it clear that not

only do these retarded youngsters have a manipulative orientation, but they can implement it with a surprising degree of skill and sophistication. They show a high concern for fate determination, and even though these young people have spent most of their lives in institutions they have not become the passive, acquiescent vegetables that so much of the literature leads us to believe. In short, these retardates did not act like retardates are *supposed to* but rather presented the picture of children prematurely exposed to a hostile environment—children who not only have the capacity and intelligence to survive, but also the ability to master and control their environment.

The question can be raised, however, whether retardates will engage in this kind of behavior outside experimental situations that are designed specifically to induce this kind of behavior. The next logical step, then, would be to explore directly the motivations, goals, attitudes, and self-conceptions of retardates and their consequences for the everyday behavior of the retardate. Thus, we turn next to an exploration of the retardates' styles of adaptation to the institution.

Styles of Adaptation
to the Training School

The typical state training school for the retarded, at first glance, appears to be an oppressive, depressing, and monolithic setting which social scientists refer to as a "total institution" (Goffman, 1961)—one in which the inmates live, work, and play, usually under the eyes of an authoritarian staff. These settings are seen as the epitome of destructive, demeaning, and dehumanizing milieus. Moreover, many share the assumption that in a "total institution" even the staunchest, most talented, and cleverest persons will succumb eventually to the mighty power of the institution, ending up as psychological vegetables. Denuded of their own personal needs, goals, and desires, they conform instead to those fostered by the institution.

In such a setting it would seem most unlikely that "defective" humans would not only attempt to resist the powers that be, but would be successful as well. This was, nonetheless, what we found in our research with mental patients (mostly schizophrenics); they lived in much the same manner as persons on the outside, doing those things that were personally satisfying, setting up their own preferred styles of life—ones which more often than not were clearly at variance with those encouraged by the institution and expected of the mental patients (Braginsky and others, 1969).

In keeping with our beliefs about defective populations in general, and here specifically about familial retardates, we expect that they too will be able to manipulate their environment in order to fulfill their personal styles of adaptation. That is, we believe that retardates follow the same laws of behavior as people in general, and that training schools, like most communities, offer to their residents alternate paths of adaptation. Thus, our model of retardate adaptation is a familiar one: (1) The needs, attitudes, goals, and interests that a person has upon entry into a new environment as well as his previously learned techniques for adaptation, determine (2) how and where he will spend his time in the new setting (that is, his *style of adaptation*), which, in turn, influences (3) what he learns about his new environment, how visible he is to other members, how long he resides there, and so on.

To illustrate this very simply, let us suppose that Joey, a boy single-mindedly interested in baseball and hoping to grow up to become a big-league player, moves to a new neighborhood. According to this model, we would expect Joey to seek out the local ball field or Little League team, spend most of his free time there, and become engaged in ball playing activities. As a result of focusing his attention almost exclusively here, he would tend to have little information concerning other aspects of his new community (for example, where the local library is or where teen-age dances are held), while at the same time he would learn a great deal about persons he plays ball with, become visible to this group, and know the game schedules and related activities in detail. Moreover, if he is very satisfied with his new adaptation, he should be reluctant to move from this community. Thus, if he had a say in the matter, he would

```
┌─────────────────────────────┐
│   Antecedent Variables      │
│                             │
│     Needs, interests,       │
│     attitudes, skills at    │
│     adaptation, and so on   │
└─────────────────────────────┘
              │
              ▼
┌─────────────────────────────────┐
│   Mediating Variables           │
│                                 │
│   ADAPTATION STYLE              │
│        │                        │
│     Referents                   │
│        ▼                        │
│  Where P spends time in community; │
│  what P does; how much time he  │
│  spends at activities, and so on │
└─────────────────────────────────┘
              │
              ▼
┌─────────────────────────────┐
│   Consequence Variables     │
│                             │
│     Information about        │
│     community, length        │
│     of residency, visibility │
│     to community members,    │
│     and so on                │
└─────────────────────────────┘
```

tend to want to remain a resident in this new, personally satisfying neighborhood.

On the other hand, Joey's sister, Mary, has studied ballet for several years and wants to become a great ballerina. To her dismay she finds that there are no adequate facilities in her new neighborhood or in the nearby vicinity for her to pursue her burning interest in dance. Consequently, she should want to leave this community in order to seek out a locale where she can adapt in a more personally satisfying way. If she had a say in the matter, her family would move tomorrow.

With respect to persons residing in the institutions for the retarded, however, a qualifying comment which does not alter the content or structure of the model must be added. A number of training-school residents had been admitted to the training schools at very early ages (six months through four years). For them this milieu is the only one with which they are familiar, just as many persons spend their adult lives in the town or neighborhood where they were born and raised. We expect, therefore, that these persons will live in the institution in a similar way that we all live in our communities.

If we are correct in our assertions, then we should be able to uncover, upon examining how "retardates" live in the training school, not one institutionally prescribed style of life but several different styles of adaptation. The model we have presented enables us to investigate this hypothesis in three ways: by examining (1) the presumed antecedent variables (needs, attitudes, and so on); (2) the consequence variables (information acquisition, visibility, and so on), or, more directly, (3) the referents associated with the mediating variable, style of adaptation (where and how they spend their time). Since the first two approaches would offer merely indirect evidence, necessitating inference beyond the data, the first study to be presented will involve direct inquiry into how the residents live in the institution. The studies that follow will be used to investigate the relationships, if any, that exist between the antecedent, mediating, and consequence variables.

Stated more formally, the specific predictions that we will be dealing with in this order are:

1. "Retardates" differ in their styles of adaptation to the training school.

2. Styles of adaptation are related to "retardate" attitudes about mental retardation, the training school, and being a resident there.

3. Styles of adaptation are related to the kinds of information "retardates" acquire about the training school.

4. Styles of adaptation are related to the length of institutionalization.

5. Styles of adaptation are *not* related to indices of intelligence or to differential demands of the institution.

"RETARDATE" STYLES OF ADAPTATION

In order to find out how "retardates" live in the training school, we went directly to the source, the "retardates." A structured interview schedule (tape recorded for later analyses) was administered individually to 175 residents in the two state institutions (100 from training school F; 75 from training school M), with almost an equal representation of males and females.

Each "retardate" was asked to describe in detail how and where he spent his waking hours for both a typical day during the week and a typical day on weekends. Four scores were assigned for the typical week day based on the number of hours spent (a) at school, (b) on the ward, unit, or in the cottage, (c) at work, and (d) off the ward in informal social activities. Since there is no school on weekends, only the latter three categories were used for the typical weekend day. These categories accounted for almost all of the residents' responses.

In addition to the styles of adaptation information, we also included questions to assess: (1) *Perceived Institution Demands*—"Where *must* you spend time in the training school; where are you *ordered* to go?" "What activities must you engage in?" "How much time *must* you spend there?" These questions permit us not only to examine the residents' perception of the institutions' demands but later to determine whether differential demands are associated with different styles of adaptation. (2) *Psychological Ecology of the Institution*— "Name the places in the training school where a retardate can spend time." "What can he do there?" "What do residents usually do there?" From this information the perceived number and kinds of pathways for adaptation as well as the "richness" of the milieu can be determined. (3) *"Retardate" Motility*— The focus here is on the degree to which the residents perceive their movements as being restricted by the training school. "Where *can't* you go or spend time in the training school?" "What places are *off limits* to the residents and why?" The number and kinds of locations mentioned can be indices of the intensity and extent of resident restriction.

Hypothesis 1: "Retardates" differ in their styles of adaptation to the training school.

Since most of the residents' week-day waking hours are filled with compulsory activities, this information could not be used to test our hypothesis, which presupposes the element of choice and "free time." For example, almost all of the familial-cultural retardates under sixteen years were required to spend six hours in school, followed by compulsory work assignments, dinner, and restriction to their unit in the evening. (Later in this chapter a description of the "typical" day of the "typical" resident will be presented in detail.) On the weekend, however, some of the prescribed activities and restrictions are formally or informally loosened. Thus, a more accurate assessment of resident styles of adaptation can be made by examining where and how residents choose to spend their relatively free time during the weekend.

The index of styles of adaptation for individuals was derived by comparing each resident's weekend time to the median time for the other residents on three categories: (a) at work, (b) on the ward, or (c) socializing off the ward. Thus, we wished to determine which residents spent more time at the various activities than most (50 percent) of the others, and which spent less time than most.

These indexes were computed separately for each institution, since the average time spent on the ward and off the ward socializing varied from training school to training school. At training school M, the average amount of time spent on the ward was 10.25 hours; off the ward socializing, 1.42 hours; and at work, 1.01 hours. The corresponding times spent at training school F were: 6.47 hours on the ward; 4.07 hours socializing; and 1.46 hours at work.

Twenty-five of the residents (14 percent) usually were not at the training school on weekends. The results, based on the 150 who spent their weekends on the institutions' grounds, were: 11 percent spent more time than most at work and spent less time on the ward or off the ward socializing; 17 percent spent more than the median amount of time on the ward and less time at work or off the ward socializing; 29 percent were above the median on time spent off the ward socializing and were below the median for work and ward time. Thus the majority of the residents (58 per cent) exhibited "pure" styles of adaptation, showing clear preferences for being "warders," "workers," or "mobile socializers." The remaining 42 percent manifested variants of the combinations of these three types. It is noteworthy that similar results were obtained with the mental patients we studied (see Braginsky and others, 1969), 65 percent of whom were "pure" types with 19 percent being "workers," 21 percent "warders," and 25 percent "socializers."

It is clear by now that this hypothesis has been supported by the data. "Retardates" not only showed individual differences in how they chose to live in the institution, but they manifested clearly identifiable styles of adaptation.

Before we proceed to examine how these styles of adaptation are related to attitudes, information acquisition, and the other variables in question, a few words concerning some demographic differences between warders, workers, and socializers are in order. Although there were no cross-institutional differences for each style of adaptation, there were some rather striking differences between the groups with respect to age and sex. For example, a brief look at Table 10 discloses that the average age of the socializers was significantly less than the warders' age, who in turn were younger than the workers ($F = 8.75$, $p < .001$). When we view this finding in the context of community life in general, it is not particularly unusual to find that the younger members gad about more readily than the older ones.

TABLE 10

Mean Age of Warders, Workers, and Socializers

	WARDERS	WORKERS	SOCIALIZERS
Mean	21.50	24.35	17.45
S.D.	6.31	6.98	5.75

The sex composition of the groups also tends to reflect the styles of adaptation of males and females in our society. The warders, similar to "homebodies," are mostly girls (73 percent), whereas the socializers, those who stray from where they are "supposed" to be, are primarily boys (80 percent). Although sex differences in group composition are significant for the warders and socializers ($x^2 = 18.86$, $p < .001$), there were no such differences for the workers (53 percent girls, 47 percent boys).

THE ATTITUDES OF THE WARDERS, WORKERS, AND SOCIALIZERS

We posited earlier that one's attitudes are reflected to a large extent in one's style of adaptation. Although we assume in our model that attitudes represent an antecedent variable, admittedly there is no way for us to determine, for this population, if the attitudes truly preceded the style of adaptation or vice versa. In any case, let us attempt to examine the relationships that may exist between a retardate's attitudes about his "affliction," about the institution, and about dwelling there and his style of adaptation to the training school.

In order to assess these attitudes, a test similar to the one we employed with mental patients was constructed. The attitude questionnaires were administered individually to each retardate, who was requested to respond either "true" or "false" to each statement. Items designed to ascertain attitudes toward mental retardation included statements such as: "Once a retardate, always a retardate"; "There is nothing wrong with being retarded"; "All retardates in institutions should be prevented from having children by a painless operation." A few examples of items used to tap attitudes toward the training school are: "In many ways living here is like living in any other neighborhood you would find"; "One of the best spots in this place is the canteen"; "Retardates would get better if matrons and attendants did not bother them so much." The items dealing with attitudes toward being institutionalized included: "If I get to live outside, I will try to hide that I was a retardate here"; "A person would be foolish not to try to enjoy himself as long as he is in the state school"; "It is important not to think about the life you could lead outside this place as long as you are here." A complete copy of the 100-item Retardate Attitude Test (RAT) can be found in Appendix B.

Hypothesis 2: Styles of adaptation are related to "retardate" attitudes about mental retardation, the training school, and being a resident there.

To investigate the validity of this hypothesis, first the percent of agreement (true responses) for each RAT item was determined separately for warders, workers, and socializers. Comparisons between pairs of the groups (that is, between warders and workers, warders and socializers, socializers and workers) on the percentages obtained for each item were subjected to a statistical test in order to distinguish the items on which the groups differed significantly. Since a total of 300 comparisons were made, by using the usual 5 percent level of significance one could expect 15 comparisons to be significantly different on the basis of chance alone. A more stringent criteria, therefore, was used to determine significant differences ($p <$ .025).

The results showed that 80 of the comparisons (27 percent) differentiated between the groups: 33 items were significantly different for socializers and workers, 27 items for warders and socializers, and 20 items for warders and workers. There was divergence between these groups on 51 of the 100 items. These items as well as the scores obtained by each group are reported in Table 11.

It should be noted here that on only 8 of the 80 significant items did one of the groups tend to agree with an item while the other group tended to disagree. Thus, most of the differences are in terms of the magnitude of agreement or disagreement, rather than in holding contradictory attitudes. For instance, although all three groups agreed that "a retardate should make his life as simple as possible" in the training school, more workers endorsed this item (94 percent) than socializers (77 percent).

TABLE 11

Percent Agreement on RAT Items by Adaptation Styles

ITEM	$N = 26$ (W) WARDERS	$N = 17$ (K) WORKERS	$N = 44$ (S) SOCIALIZERS	SIGNIFICANT DIFFERENCE BETWEEN
1. More money should be spent by people in the care and treatment of retardates.	81	94	79	S–K*
2. Anyone who tries hard to better himself deserves the respect of others.	88	82	74	W–S*
3. If this place had enough well-trained people working here, many of the retardates would improve enough to get out of the school.	92	100	84	S–K**
4. It is better to be a person who is unimportant and honest than to be one who is important and dishonest.	77	76	58	S–K*; W–S*
5. A person would be foolish not to try to enjoy himself as long as he is in the state school.	65	53	81	S–K**; W–S*
6. In many ways living here is just like living in any other neighborhood you would find.	85	59	67	W–S*; W–K**

7. The superintendent of this school should try hard to get attendants who are able to get along with the retardates.	100	94	86	W–S**
8. It is important not to think about the life you could lead outside this place as long as you live here.	69	71	51	S–K*; W–S**
9. More than anything else, the retardates need the respect and understanding of the people who work with them.	96	100	91	S–K*
10. Although retardates may seem all right when they have left here, they should not be allowed to marry.	35	53	28	S–K**
11. Regardless of how you look at it, retardates are no longer really human.	27	47	21	S–K**
12. Once a retardate, always a retardate.	27	35	49	W–S**
13. It's important for a retardate to have a sense of humor.	81	82	65	S–K*; W–S*
14. Never tell anyone the real reason you did something unless it will be helpful to you.	65	94	63	S–K**; W–K**
15. There is little that can be done for a retardate here except to see that he is comfortable and well-fed.	77	94	86	W–K*

TABLE 11 (cont'd)

ITEM	$N = 26$ (W) WARDERS	$N = 17$ (K) WORKERS	$N = 44$ (S) SOCIALIZERS	SIGNIFICANT DIFFERENCE BETWEEN
16. All retardates in institutions should be prevented from having children by a painless operation.	54	29	44	W–K*
17. There are many people on the outside more disturbed than retardates who have been here for a long time.	92	71	63	W–S**; W–K**
18. People who were once retardates here are no more dangerous than anyone else.	73	88	63	S–K**
19. People should be sure they are doing the right thing before they do it.	96	76	81	W–S**; W–K**
20. A retardate should try to make his life as simple as possible in this place.	85	94	77	S–K**
21. Retardates should spend time getting to know more about themselves by sitting down alone and thinking.	96	65	93	S–K**; W–K**
22. Most retardates in this place are willing to work.	92	100	88	S–K**

23. If I had grown up in a normal home, I wouldn't be here.	69	94	67	S–K**; W–K**
24. You have to get to know your matron if you want to get out of this place.	92	94	79	S–K**; W–S*
25. The best way to get help for your problems is to keep busy and forget you are a retardate.	92	100	70	S–K**; W–S**
26. Retardates here should have as much freedom as they want.	92	100	77	S–K**; W–S*
27. Even if a retardate who had been here seems better, he should not be given a driver's license.	31	71	35	S–K**; W–K**
28. I don't think there should be places like this, but only ones where you don't live in.	69	59	44	W–S**
29. When a person has a problem or a worry, it is best not to think about it, but keep busy with more pleasant things.	85	94	70	S–K**; W–S*
30. The only hope for a retardate here is to get understanding.	88	88	72	S–K*; W–S*
31. The law should allow a woman to divorce her husband as soon as he has been in a place like this.	54	29	37	W–K*

TABLE 11 (cont'd)

ITEM	$N = 26$ (W) WARDERS	$N = 17$ (K) WORKERS	$N = 44$ (S) SOCIALIZERS	SIGNIFICANT DIFFERENCE BETWEEN
32. The main purpose of a state school for the retarded should be to protect the public from retarded people.	81	65	47	W–S**
33. Everyone should have someone in his life whose happiness means as much to him as his own.	92	88	74	W–S**
34. A retardate should get to know the people who work here before he starts to get treated for his condition.	85	76	67 •	W–S*
35. A retardate should never leave here until he is completely well.	81	94	58	S–K**; W–S**
36. The thing most retardates here need is a period of relaxation to get on their feet again.	92	82	72	W–S**; W–K*
37. If you want to get better, it's important to establish a comfortable routine here.	92	94	74	S–K**; W–S**
38. If I get to live outside, I will try to hide that I was a retardate here.	88	76	58	S–K*; W–S**
				W–S**; W–K**

40. A retardate can't improve unless he is prepared to suffer a little.	65	88	56	S–K**; W–K**
41. You should try to be on friendly terms with the attendants and matrons.	100	82	91	W–S**; W–K**
42. It would be good for retardates if this place told them what to do all the time.	50	35	56	S–K*
43. Retardates would get better if matrons and attendants did not bother them so much.	77	94	74	S–K**; W–K**
44. Everybody has a little bit wrong with them.	85	94	77	S–K**
45. You can be sure that most people have a mean streak and they will show it whenever they have the chance.	88	100	79	S–K**; W–K*
46. Retardates should be permitted to go into town whenever they want to.	88	53	74	S–K*; W–S*; W–K**
47. It's a smart thing to be nice to important people.	100	94	84	W–S**
48. Honesty is always the best policy.	77	100	74	S–K**; W–K**
49. There are good reasons for lying sometimes.	58	82	60	S–K*; W–K*
50. It is hard to get ahead without cheating.	73	76	58	S–K*
51. Most people who work here really don't know what we do at this place.	62	82	72	W–K*

$*$ $p < .025$
$**$ $p < .01$

Yet despite the similarity in the direction of the response, the differences become more striking when we consider the homogeneity of attitudes for all the 177 retardates questioned. A correlation computed between the attitude profiles of the 100 retardates at Training School F and of the 77 retardates at Training School M showed an extremely high relationship between their responses ($r = .93$, $p < .001$). Thus, despite the uniformity of retardates' attitudes, the warders, workers, and socializers are divergent in their attitude profile. Some of these differences obviously are related to their particular styles of adaptation. For example, one almost expects socializers more so than the other two groups to agree that "a person would be foolish not to try to enjoy himself as long as he is in the state school," since this appears to be how he lives. On the other hand, more workers, who because of their tasks seem to have the least "fun," would be expected to endorse the belief that "a retardate can't improve unless he is prepared to suffer a little," while fewer warders and even fewer socializers would agree.

We still, however, have no evidence that these attitudinal differences precede (are antecedents of) the style of adaptation to the training school. One bit of data which indirectly bears upon this question is the relationship between length of institutionalization and attitudes. That is, if it is living in the institution that forms one's attitudes, how long one lives there should be related to at least some of the items. The correlations computed between the number of years spent in the institution and the 100 items, however, indicate no relationship. More specifically, not one attitude item was significantly related to length of institutionalization.

More direct support for our assumption that attitudes are antecedents of styles of adaptation was obtained in our studies with the "mentally ill." In short, whether these attitudes precede, interact with, or are outcomes of institutional styles of life, our hypothesis has been confirmed: styles of adaptation are significantly related to attitudes.

INFORMATION ACQUISITION, AND STYLES
OF ADAPTATION

Since it is impossible, of course, to learn everything about one's environment, people tend to be selective in the kinds of information they acquire. This is most readily seen when a person enters a new and different milieu, as in our example of Joey and his sister, Mary. Thus a great deal of the information we obtain, as well as that which we neglect to obtain, is based on our needs, interests, goals, and so on. In terms of the model presented earlier, much of what one learns about his environment is one of the many outcomes of one's style of adaptation.

Although this is so very obvious when one considers "normal" persons, mentally retarded individuals are usually excluded from simple formulations of human behavior. Thus it was deemed important to demonstrate not only for theoretical purposes (that is, to test the model), but also to emphasize the basic humanness of retardates, that retardate styles of adaptation are differentially related to the kinds of information they acquire.

A 35 item test was constructed in order to measure two general areas of knowledge about the training school: information about the staff members and about the residential aspects of the institution. Fourteen items dealt with the names of important staff members and the location of their offices; 16 items were concerned with residential information such as the names and locations of buildings as well as the activities that go on in them. There were five items dealing with miscellaneous questions such as: "What time does the night shift start?" "How many retardates are there in this training school?"

Each item on the Information Test (IT) was selected on the basis of these criteria: (1) the answers had to be potentially obvious, so that retardates would not have had to acquire exotic information about the training school in order to respond correctly; (2) the information could be learned without the retardate having to make personal contact with the staff.

Hypothesis 3: Styles of adaptation are related to the kinds of information "retardates" acquire about the training school.

The number of correct responses to the IT were computed for each subject. The mean scores obtained by the warders, workers, and socializers with respect to People, Place, and Total Information are shown in Table 12. Analyses of variance of these data indicated that workers and, to a lesser extent, warders had significantly more knowledge about the important staff members of the training school than did the socializers ($F = 6.30$, $p < .005$). In addition, the workers knew significantly more about the institution in general than the warders, who in turn had more total information than the socializers ($F = 5.19$, $p < .005$). It is of interest to note that although the socializers are less informed about the staff at the training school, they have no such deficit with information concerning the residential aspects of the institution. On these items they do as well as the other two groups. Thus the lower total information score of the socializers is the result of their lack of knowledge about the personnel at the training school, rather than about what goes on at the various buildings on the premises.

A close look at Table 13, however, seems to indicate some inconsistencies with respect to the knowledge of the socializers. Specifically, fewer socializers know the number and locations of canteens as well as where the dances are held, than do the

TABLE 12

Mean Scores for People, Place, and Total Information

	PEOPLE	PLACE	TOTAL
Warders	7.54	8.92	18.73
Workers	8.41	8.65	21.88
Socializers	5.86	8.61	16.43

warders and workers. To clarify this, it should be mentioned that the canteens are not intended for the retardates' use but are instead for the staff. The question dealing with where the dances are held was incorrectly answered by 23 percent of this group primarily because they are rather young and, therefore, are not allowed to attend the dances. Thus, their lack of this information does not reflect a lack of sociability, but rather a larger representation of young retardates (twelve through fifteen) in this group as compared to warders and workers.

These findings parallel what one would expect to find in any community. The workers, the residents who have the most staff contact and the most amount of "legitimate" freedom of movement, should know more about their community than the younger socializers and warders. The socializers, who no doubt have a stake in being "invisible" to the staff (a point which will be elaborated upon shortly) so that they may leave their unit unsupervised in order to socialize informally with other residents, should know less about the staff than the warders, who hang around their unit and cannot help but make contact with the staff.

Additional confirmatory evidence that warders, workers, and socializers acquire different kinds of information is offered by the item-by-item analysis presented in Table 13. Twenty-seven of the original 35 items were found to be comparable for both institutions, and it was on these items only that comparisons were made between the percentage of correct responses for warders, workers, and socializers.

A total of 81 comparisons were made between the obtained percentages, 36 (44 percent) of which significantly differentiated between pairs of the groups. The greatest number of differences were between the socializers and workers (16 items), followed by the differences between warders and socializers (12 items), and finally the least between the warders and workers (8 items). These differences in information acquisition follow closely those found for attitude profiles, where again the greatest discrepancy was between workers and socializers, then socializers and warders, and last between workers and warders.

TABLE 13

*Percent Correct Responses
on Information Test*

ITEM	$N=26$ (W) WARDERS	$N=17$ (K) WORKERS	$N=44$ (S) SOCIALIZERS	SIGNIFICANT DIFFERENCES BETWEEN
1. Name of a physician at the training school.	81	76	64	W–S**
2. Building of his office.	62	59	30	W–S***; S–K***
3. Name of a nurse.	62	35	27	W–K***; W–S***
4. Location of her office.	58	82	30	W–K***; W–S***
5. Name of a matron.	96	100	91	S–K**
6. Location of her office.	81	82	95	W–S***; S–K**
7. Name of attendant in building.	96	100	98	—
8. Name of a psychologist.	12	35	20	W–K***
9. Location of his office.	42	59	30	S–K***
10. Name of a social worker.	46	65	34	S–K***
11. Name of head of training school.	65	94	61	W–K***; S–K***
12. Number of floors in your building.	88	71	73	W–K°; W–S***

13. Building closest to the administration building.	23	59	50	W–K***; W–S***
14. Is building A closer than C to building B?	65	82	80	W–S*
15. Number of canteens.	88	94	80	S–K**
16. Buildings where canteens are located.	62	71	48	S–K***
17. Where are dances held?	92	100	77	W–S**; S–K***
18. Number of people living in your building.	31	24	20	—
19. Where are movies shown?	92	100	73	W–S***; S–K***
20. Number of retardates at training school.	4	12	0	S–K***
21. Time of evening shift.	77	94	82	W–K**; S–K*
22. Building where employees live.	69	94	50	W–K***; W–S***; S–K***
23. Who is head of the social workers?	12	18	5	S–K**
24. Who is head of the nurses?	31	35	5	W–S***; S–K***
25. Who is head of the psychology department?	0	0	5	—
26. Where is the main switchboard?	46	65	45	S–K**
27. Amount of vacation attendants get.	27	29	27	—

$* \ p < .05$
$** \ p < .025$
$*** \ p < .01$

Thus on the basis of several analyses of the information test data, our hypothesis has been strongly confirmed: styles of adaptation are related to the types and amounts of information retardates acquire about the training school.

LENGTH OF RESIDENCY AND STYLES
OF ADAPTATION

It might be argued by some that just as styles of adaptation are influenced by sex and age, so too may they be influenced by how long one lives in a community. We have stated, to the contrary, that length of residency, to a large extent, is an *outcome*—not an *antecedent*—of styles of adaptation. Thus if a community is found to lack the qualities necessary for one's personal fulfillment, a person will be likely to leave that community in search of a more favorable one. Surely, the residents of the training school have no comparable freedom of movement to enter or leave their communities. The steps they must take, the formulas they must follow, the skills they must have, and the age they must reach before they can leave the training school have been formally prescribed by the State. Yet we maintain that even in the light of all the institutional deterrents to discharge, styles of adaptation will be a major determinant of the length of institutionalization.

Let us see first if, in fact, styles of adaptation are related to length of residency, and then try to determine the nature of the relationship.

Hypothesis 4: Styles of adaptation are related to the length of institutionalization.

The number of years spent in the training school are reported in Table 14 separately for warders, workers, and socializers. The analysis of these data show that there is a significant difference in length of residency for the three groups ($F = 4.76$, $p < .025$), with workers having spent the most amount of time living in the training school, socializers the least, and warders falling in between the two. Since the order of the groups' number of years in residence parallels the order of their respective ages (workers are the oldest, socializers the youngest, and warders in between), it might appear that the workers, for example, have spent more time in the training school only because they are older. It should be pointed out, however, that the percent of one's life spent in the institution is not significantly different for the three groups (see Table 14). That is, although the three groups have not spent the same absolute amount of time in the training school, they have all spent about one half of their lives there. Age alone, therefore, cannot account for the differences in length of residency.

A subsidiary finding, not at all predicted, needs explanation: that socializers enter the institution at a significantly earlier age than the warders, and especially the workers ($F = 7.36$, $p < .005$). One possible explanation is that the socializers are more "retarded" than the other groups, and, as a result, they were recognized and sent to the training school earlier in their lives. Their style of adaptation would, therefore, reflect their retardation rather than the motivational system we posited.

TABLE 14

*Mean Number of Years and Percent
of Life in the Training School*

	WARDERS	WORKERS	SOCIALIZERS
Number of years			
Mean	9.27	13.59	8.66
S.D.	4.84	7.41	5.41
Percent of life			
Mean	42.96	52.35	45.39
S.D.	16.82	18.20	17.87
Age at admission			
Mean	11.80	10.76	8.84
S.D.	4.74	3.10	2.29

The data to be presented shortly (see Hypothesis 5), however, forces us to discount completely this interpretation.

Another possible explanation involves the age of admission as a partial determinant of styles of adaptation. The workers and warders, who are about thirteen years old upon entry to the institution, may be seen as potentially more troublesome than the younger entrants, among them the socializers. To simmer whatever sinister impulses the staff may believe the adolescents have, this group would be kept under tighter control than the younger ones. This is not very different from the way many parents deal with their blooming adolescent children, who they fear may be headed toward the use of drugs and sexual abandonment, and, for girls in particular, the fear of pregnancy. As we shall see in later chapters, many of the adolescent girls are sent to the training school after having been "in trouble" sexually. This may well account for tighter restrictions on the girls' units, leading many potential socializers by force to become warders. The over-representation of girls (73 percent) in our warder group and their striking under-representation in the socializer group (20 percent) may indeed reflect external restrictions. This position is given more credence when we investigate the activities that the girls engage in while on the ward, as opposed to those which the boys on the ward engage in. Most of the girls reported that they spent most of their time on the ward interacting with other residents or with staff members. The boys, on the other hand, spent their time in solitary activities such as reading or watching television. Thus within this style of adaptation we find a striking sex difference, one which again reflects sex differences found in society at large.

As we shall see shortly, the workers and the warders represent styles of adaptation which are approved of by the institution; these residents are under constant supervision and always within eyesight. It is the socializers who subvert one of the major aims of the training school, by slipping out of their units and socializing in unsupervised areas of the institution.

We do not mean to imply here that warders and workers are succumbing to institutional demands rather than following, to a large extent, their own desired styles of adaptation. Indeed, it seems as though these two groups represent retardates who also have aims that are counter—albeit more subtly—to the training school's espoused goals. The majority of the workers, for example, have reached the legal age and have learned the necessary skills for living on the outside (the goal of the training school for their "educables"); they have not, however, taken the necessary steps to seek discharge from the institution. Those who are somehow "forced" to leave by a friendly and enthusiastic social worker, very often return after a brief sojourn into the community at large. Implicit in our discussion here is that we believe there are a large number of retardates who can—but who do not want to—leave the institution. This phenomenon has been observed in institutionalized adult populations (see Braginsky, *et al.*, 1969), but has been encountered rarely with younger persons. It is, perhaps, best summed up by the retardate we interviewed who had just returned to the institution after a brief discharge period: "You really work hard out there, and you don't get much money. Then when you go to enjoy yourself, you need lots of money —it's really tough out there. The younger kids here think that life is great on the outside, but we older ones who've been out there know how tough it is."

Perhaps the most parsimonious explanation of the discrepancies in age between our groups, particularly the under-representation of adult socializers (over twenty-one), is that the socializers, when they are allowed, leave the institution more readily than the warders and workers. Indeed, we have suggested throughout this chapter that it is the socializers whose style of adaptation conflicts most overtly with the desired styles of the training school. Since the socializers' personal satisfactions can be met only through great effort and subterfuge, it would be expected that when given the opportunity they would choose to leave that community.

Although a number of questions still require documentation and less interpretation, our formal hypothesis that styles of adaptation are related to length of residency has been supported.

OTHER DETERMINANTS OF STYLES
OF ADAPTATION

There are those who, despite the preceding evidence, will maintain still that the styles of adaptation we have documented may be merely the function of the retardates' level of intelligence, differential demands of the training school, and/or an interaction between the two. If one believes that the retardate is a "defective" human being and that the institution is an omniscient structure, these explanations are very real and more than plausible; they conveniently assist in the maintenance of the "myth."

There is no need at this point to reiterate our position. Let us turn to the data to compare the validity of our position with the above interpretation. The data relevant to the differential demands notion were obtained in the interviews described earlier from the sections dealing with (1) Perceived Institution Demands, (2) Psychological Ecology of the Institution, and (3) Retardate Motility. The data concerning the level of intelligence were obtained from the institutions' records, which included a summary diagnostic level of intelligence ranging from 1 (borderline) to 4 (severe or profound retardation) for each retardate.

Hypothesis 5: Styles of adaptation are not related to indexes of intelligence or to differential demands of the institution.

To the questions dealing with institutional demands, psychological ecology, and retardate motility, there was an unforeseen uniformity of response. That is, when the retardates we interviewed were asked: "Where *must* you spend time in the training school?" "Where *can* you spend time?" and "What *places* are off-limits?" they all responded with robot-like similarity: they must go to the activities to which they are assigned (for example, school or work), they must return directly to their unit, and everything is off-limits unless special permission or staff supervision is available. In short, the training school de-

TABLE 15

*Mean Intelligence Level of Warders,
Workers, and Socializers*

	WARDERS	WORKERS	SOCIALIZERS
Mean	2.27	2.18	1.93
S.D.	.66	.81	.69

mands are restrictive and authoritarian, but, more important
to our hypothesis, they are uniform for all residents. Thus
one cannot explain the differences in styles of adaptation as a
function of different institutional demands made upon the
residents; the formal restrictions were the same for all the
retardates in our study.

The mean level of intelligence of the warders, workers, and
socializers, presented in Table 15, clearly discredits any interpretation of styles of adaptation based on intellectual functioning. The three groups were not only similar to each other, but
they were representative of the entire sample of 177.

Our hypothesis, that differential institutional demands and
levels of intelligence are unrelated to retardate styles of adaptation, therefore, stands confirmed.

SUMMARY AND DISCUSSION

To summarize our findings concerning styles of adaptation,
three main styles were identified: "warders," "workers," and
"mobile socializers." Moreover, each of these styles was associated with a different kind of retardate with respect to present
age, age at admission, sex, and kinds of attitudes about retardation, the training school, and being a resident there. As
we anticipated, styles of adaptation were related to different
institutional outcomes, such as information acquired about the
staff and residential aspects of the training school, and length

of residency. Of particular interest, the styles of adaptation were unrelated to indexes of intellectual functioning and to direct institutional pressures.

Thus, our assertion, and, in fact, the crucial underpinning of our research—that institutionalized cultural-familial retardates can be understood in terms usually reserved for "normal" people—has been firmly supported by the results. Throughout this chapter we have employed the same constructs and assumptions used in understanding the interaction between normal persons and their communities to understand the relationship between the retardate and his community, the training school. The relationships that were predicted by our model made no recourse to assumptions concerning the dynamics of retardation or of institutional power.

The findings did not offer a modicum of evidence for the traditional belief that retardates are functionally different from people in general, particularly young people. They were no more helpless, inadequate, stupid, or less able to control their fates than their noninstitutionalized counterparts. Instead, the results showed that the retardates were successful in utilizing their environment to their satisfaction; that they initiated and maintained the life styles they valued personally, even when these styles were at variance with the institutionally valued ones.

Two rather illuminating facets about institutionalized retardates have thus far been uncovered. First, we have shown that they are rather effective human beings, capable of using subtle forms of counterpower (such as impression management) in order to meet their needs. Second, we have demonstrated that, within the confines of a restrictive institution, they can promote their own life styles. We consider these findings important not only from a theoretical point of view but also because they generate a new kind of insight into the behavior of "retardates" precluded by the traditional perspective of mental retardation.

The bulk of our research in this chapter has been concerned primarily with the individual differences among retardates. But if we adhere to our basic assumption that retardates are like people in general, we should expect to find similarities among them just as we expect to find similarities among any group of persons living together for a large part of their lives in the same community.

THE MODAL MENTAL RETARDATE

Here we stress the term "modal" rather than "average" retardate, since we are not concerned with the statistical average of retardate characteristics (which so often do not represent even one person), but instead with the characteristics most retardates share. The purpose of such a portrayal is twofold: first, it would be illuminating to know, over and above individual variation, what beliefs, attitudes, kinds of information, and styles of life are common to the institutionalized retardates in our study. Second, in the next chapter this portrait of the retardate will enable us to compare his modal attitudes with those held by the professional and subprofessional staff at the training schools. This comparison should yield information concerning the conflict between retardates and the representatives of the institution to which we have alluded throughout the book.

MODAL INFORMATION ACQUISITION

The percentage of correct responses to the Information Test for all 177 subjects can be seen in Table 16. In general, the retardates have more information about the residential aspects of the training school than about the staff: 90 percent know where dances are held, 89 percent where movies are shown, 88 percent the number of canteens, while only 46 percent know the name of a nurse, and 14 percent the name of a psychologist. Moreover, there is a striking difference in the information retardates have about the professional and subprofessional staff. As one would expect, more retardates know the staff members with whom they have direct personal contact, the attendants and matrons. While 98 percent know the name of an attendant in their building and 94 percent the

TABLE 16

Percentage of Correct Responses to Information Test
$(N = 177)$

ITEMS	PERCENT
1. Name of a physician at training school.	76
2. Building of his office.	53
3. Name of a nurse.	46
4. Where is her office?	54
5. Name of a matron.	94
6. Where is her office?	91
7. Name of attendant in building.	98
8. Name of a psychologist.	14
9. Where is his office?	36
10. Name of a social worker.	55
11. Name of head of training school.	71
12. Number of floors in your building.	81
13. Building closest to administration building.	48
14. Is building A closer than C to building B?	77
15. Number of canteens.	88
16. Buildings where canteens are located.	59
17. Where are dances held?	90
18. Number of people living in your building.	37
19. Where are movies shown?	89
20. Number of retardates at training school.	3
21. Time of evening shift.	88
22. Building where employees live.	66
23. Who is head of the social workers?	12
24. Who is head of the nurses?	15
25. Who is head of the psychology department?	2
26. Where is the main switchboard?	60
27. Amount of vacation attendants get.	41

name of a matron, 55 percent know the name of a social worker, 46 percent the name of a nurse, 15 percent the head of nurses, and 12 percent the head of social workers. Thus one can almost construct the staff hierarchy by determining their visibility to the retardates, an exception being the Head (Superintendent) of the training school.

MODAL ATTITUDES AND BELIEFS

The high degree of similarity in retardate responses to the attitude items, the homogeneity we described earlier, is reflected clearly by the number of items on which at least 70 percent of the retardates are in concordance (either agree or disagree with an item). Using this criterion, 56 of the 100 items could be considered modal. Table 17 presents those items on which there was at least 70 percent agreement among the 177 retardates, omitting the Mach items.

A perusal of this table indicates that the retardates: (1) desire a comfortable, laissez-faire, and nondemanding milieu; for example, 83 percent believe that a retardate should make his life in the training school as simple as possible, and 80 percent think that they would get better if the matrons and attendants did not bother them so much. (2) They want to enjoy their stay at the training school, reflected by their 81 percent agreement that the best way to fit in is to have a good time. (3) They do not see themselves as particularly defective or very different from people in general; for example, 82 percent think that most retardates are not as stupid as most people think, 89 percent feel that everyone has a little bit of something wrong with him, and 77 percent believe that many people on the outside are more disturbed than retardates. (4) They want to have the civil and social liberties that people in outside communities enjoy: 86 percent believe that anyone who tries to better himself deserves the respect of others, 87 percent feel that they should have as much freedom as they desire, and 77 percent want to have some say in how the training school is run. (5) They readily recognize the human condition of loneliness and the need for human relatedness: 79

TABLE 17

Modal Retardate Attitudes
$(N = 177)$

AGREE

1. More money should be spent by people in the care and treatment of retardates.

2. Anyone who tries hard to better himself deserves the respect of others.

3. If this place had enough well-trained people working here, many of the retardates would improve enough to leave.

4. The head of this school should try hard to get attendants who are able to get along with the retardates.

5. More than anything else, the retardates need the respect and understanding of the people who work with them.

6. The best things this school can do for a retardate cannot help him unless he also tries to help himself.

7. The best way to fit into this place is to have a good time.

8. There is little that can be done for a retardate here except to see that he is comfortable and well-fed.

9. A retardate should try to make his life as simple as possible in this place.

10. Retardates should spend time getting to know more about themselves by sitting alone and thinking.

11. Most retardates in this place are willing to work.

12. You have to get to know your matron if you want to get out of this place.

13. The best way to get help for your problems is to keep busy and forget you are a retardate.

14. Retardates should have as much freedom as they want.

15. It is important to learn all about this place if you want to get things done and enjoy yourself.

16. Many retardates are capable of doing a good job (skilled labor) even though in some ways they are very disturbed.

17. When a person has a problem, it is best not to think about it but keep busy with more pleasant things.

18. Everyone should have someone in his life whose happiness means as much to him as his own.

19. One of the best spots in this place is the canteen.

20. The thing most retardates need here is a period of relaxation to get on their feet again.

21. If you want to get better, it's important to establish a comfortable routine here.

22. The best way to learn about this place is to ask retardates who have been here for some time.

23. A retardate can't improve unless he is prepared to suffer a little.

24. Retardates should be required to work while here.

25. Most retardates here are not as stupid as people think.

26. Retardates would get better if matrons and attendants did not bother them so much.

27. Everybody has a little bit of something wrong with him.

28. A retardate should try to meet as many other retardates as possible rather than just staying in his own building.

29. You should always do what the matrons and attendants tell you, even if you don't want to do it.

30. Most people are lonely.

31. It's important for a retardate to have a sense of humor.

32. Sometimes an attendant or a matron can be more important in making your stay here more comfortable than some of the big bosses in the institution.

33. Watching television is good for retardates.

34. There are many people on the outside more disturbed than retardates who have been here for a long time.

35. Retardates here should have something to say about how this place is run.

36. If I had grown up in a normal home, I wouldn't be here.

TABLE 17 (*continued*)

AGREE

37. The only hope for a retardate here is to get understanding.

38. A retardate should not think about leaving here but rather how he can get better.

39. A retardate should get to know the people who work here before he starts to get treated for his condition.

40. A retardate should never leave here unless he is completely well.

41. Retardates should have more say as to whether they should leave or stay here.

42. You should try to be on friendly terms with the attendants and matrons.

43. Retardates should be permitted to go to town whenever they want to.

DISAGREE

1. The best way to handle retardates here is to keep them behind locked doors.

2. Every state school for the retarded should be surrounded by a high fence and guards.

percent of the retardates think that most people are lonely, and 86 percent feel that everyone should have someone in his life whose happiness means as much to him as his own.

MODAL STYLE OF ADAPTATION

The mean number of hours spent at work, on the ward, and in social activities off the ward are very different for week days and weekends. During a week day about 6½ hours are spent on the ward, 6 hours at work, and less than 1½ hours off the ward socializing. Thus when allowed to leave the ward, the retardate spends his week-day time working. On weekend days, however, 8 hours are generally spent on the ward, a little over

1 hour at work, and 3 hours socializing in areas other than the ward. The work and socializing time, therefore, reverse on weekends; when the retardates are free to leave their wards, they spend most of their time at informal social activities.

It is worth repeating that while on the ward the boys and girls engage in very different activities. The girls tend to spend most of their time talking to others, while the boys generally are alone watching television, reading, or just sitting.

The portrait of the retardate as he lives in the training school, what he learns about it, and his attitudes about it are, we feel, extremely edifying. Retardates typically acquire more information about the residential aspects of the institution than about the personnel; they strive for a nondemanding, pleasant environment where they can have the freedom to enjoy their stay in the training school; they do not perceive themselves as particularly stupid or defective, or, in fact, different from most other people; they spend whatever free time they have off their wards engaging in social activities with others.

This picture is unreconcilable with most professionals' and experts' views of the typical mental retardate. Instead the interests, attitudes, needs, and resultant styles of adaptation which we have suggested have been substantiated by these data. We have shown that despite attempts at maximum institutional control, the retardates can and do take advantage of alternative avenues for adaptation. Moreover, these styles of adaptation appear to be in response to the individual retardate's system of motives rather than to the demands of the training school. The mere fact that we have demonstrated a variety of adaptational styles eliminates and renders untenable the notion that the institution is all-powerful and the inmate (especially the retardate) overwhelmed and impotent in its shadow. These data taken as a whole can neither be predicted nor adequately explained by any of the conventional psychological theories of mental retardation or the sociological theories about institutions.

We have not, however, examined a very important area of institutional life which may exert a strong influence upon the retardates: namely, the relationship between the attitudes of the staff and those of the retardates. Since many of the retardates entered the training school in their "formative" years and since most have spent nearly half their lives there, one would expect that the impact of the professional and subprofessional staff on the attitudes of the retardates would be enormous. If this is the case, many of the assertions we made concerning the struggle between the institution (that is, the representatives of it) and the retardate would be invalidated. In other words, if the retardates have internalized the standards and beliefs of the staff, there would be no real conflict.

We now turn, therefore, to an examination of the staff attitudes and their comparison to the retardates' attitude profile.

Retardates and Their Keepers: Conflict of Interests

he assumed covert ideological conflict between the retardates
nd the institutional staff is crucial to much of our interpre-
ations concerning retardate behavior. The battleground on
hich we feel the conflict occurs is not limited to questions
bout how retardates should live in the training school, but
ncompasses questions such as what is the nature of their
affliction," who are they, how should they be treated, what
re their needs, and why are they incarcerated. As we noted
arlier, the retardate, faced with a severe power disadvantage
the institution, will manifest this conflict and seek its reso-
ation (in his favor, of course) through a variety of ways.
ndeed, Chapter 3 described and illustrated some of the tactics
e retardates employ, while Chapter 4 focused upon some

of the outcomes of the retardates' use of subversive power
their styles of adaptation.

Throughout our presentation, then, we emphasized the dif
ference between institutional goals and the motivational system
of the retardates. Now we will view the interaction between
the retardate and the representatives of the training school
Is there, in fact, a conflict of interests? If so, in what arena
do the conflicts exist? These are the questions to which this
chapter is addressed.

STAFF ATTITUDES ABOUT RETARDATES

In order to ascertain the attitudes that the training school staf
maintain about mental retardation, its treatment and prognosis
and the institution, a 100-item adaptation of the Retardate
Attitude Test (RAT) was constructed. The Staff Attitude Test
(SAT) items were, for the most part, identical to the RAT
items, except where the wording was inappropriate for the
staff. For instance, item 73 of the RAT read: "If I get to live
outside, I will try to hide that I was a retardate here," while
on the Staff version it was: "If a retardate gets to live outside
he should try to hide that he was a retardate here." For
simplicity of presentation, the tables that follow will use the
RAT version of the items. A copy of the SAT, however, may
be found in Appendix B.

The staff who participated in the study ranged from the
head of professional services to the matrons and attendants
A total of 96 staff members from Training Schools M ($N = 67$
and F ($N = 39$) filled out completely the attitude question
naire. Fifty of the staff had at least a bachelor's degree (Upper
Staff) and provided services at the training schools which
involved less contact with the retardates than the 46 attendant
and matrons (Lower Staff). The presentation of our result
will include, therefore, not only a portrait of the modal staf
member but of the Upper and Lower Staff as well. (We use
the terms Upper and Lower Staff to denote only the hierarchy
as it exists in the institution, implying no value judgmen
concerning the jobs in which these persons engage.)

TABLE 18

*Correlation Cofficients
for Attitude Test Profiles*

	(1)	(2)	(3)	(4)	(5)
(1) Upper Staff—F	X				
(2) Lower Staff—F	.86	X			
(3) Retardates —F	.37	.50	X		
(4) Upper Staff—M	.92	.88	.46	X	
(5) Lower Staff—M	.83	.83	.50	.88	X
(6) Retardates —M	.42	.50	.93	.38	.49

To see if we could combine the data from the two training schools as well as to investigate the relationships that might exist between the staff members at the two institutions, correlation coefficients were computed. These are reported in Table 18. As one can see, there is a great deal of similarity in attitude profiles between the various staff categories and between the training schools. The professional or Upper Staff, in particular, are very homogeneous with respect to their attitudinal responses.

In sharp contrast to the strong relationships among the personnel are those that exist between the staff groups and the retardates. It is noteworthy that these relationships are almost identical for both Training School M and F. From the correlations alone, it is clear that there exist at least two worlds in the training school: the retardates' and the staff's. We know from the last chapter what the modal world of the retardate looks like. Let us turn, therefore, to the modal world of the staff, and then to the subgroups (Upper Staff and Lower Staff modal responses).

Using the same criterion as we did for the retardates (70 percent concordance), 54 of the 100 items are modal for the combined staff groups. Since we again omitted the Machiavellian items, Table 19 presents the 47 other modal items. The 20 items with which the staff agreed (gave true responses) are strikingly similar to 17 of the retardates' modal attitudes. The items with which the staff disagreed (gave false responses), however, present a very different picture with respect to the retardates' opinions. Here, of the 27 modal staff items only two are similar for retardates, while on 11 (more than two thirds) of the items the retardates generally disagree with the staff. The asterisked statements in Table 19 represent those items on which the staff and retardates conflict. As we shall see, these concern the areas of conflict to which we have alluded.

The attitudes that both groups agree upon deal primarily with socially desirable and platitudinal statements: "more money should be spent on retardates"; "people who try hard to better themselves deserve respect"; "you should try to be on friendly terms with the attendants and matrons"; and so on.

The attitudes on which the groups diverge, on the other hand, deal directly with aspects of living in the institution, attitudes toward it, freedom for retardates, and the nature of their "affliction." For instance, 82 percent of the retardates express strong pessimism toward the "treatment" programs at the institutions by agreeing that "little can be done for a retardate here except to see that he is well fed and comfortable." Only 7 percent of the Lower Staff agree, while not one of the Upper Staff believe this to be so.

The modal concerns of the retardates that we uncovered in the preceding chapter also stand in contradiction to the staff attitudes. The retardates' interest in a nondemanding laissez-faire milieu clearly is not shared by the staff: while 83 percent of the retardates want their lives "to be as simple as possible in the training school," only 14 percent of the Upper and 28 percent of the Lower Staff agree. Similarly, 26 percent of the Upper Staff and 22 percent of the Lower agree that "retardates would get better if the attendants and matrons did not bother them so much," while 80 percent of the retardates agree.

Personal freedom for the retardate seems to be another battleground: 71 percent of the retardates think that the

TABLE 19

Modal Staff Attitudes

AGREE

---

1. More money should be spent by people in the care and treatment of retardates.

2. Anyone who tries hard to better himself deserves the respect of others.

3. If this place had enough well-trained people working here, many of the retardates would improve enough to leave.

4. A person would be foolish not to try to enjoy himself as long as he is in the state school.

5. The head of this school should try hard to get attendants who are able to get along with the retardates.

6. The best things this school can do for a retardate cannot help him unless he also tries to help himself.

7. More than anything else, the retardates need the respect and understanding of the people who work with them.

8. It is possible to have a good life here.

9. It's important for a retardate to have a sense of humor.

10. There is nothing wrong with being retarded.

11. There are many people on the outside more disturbed than retardates who have been here for a long time.

12. Sometimes an attendant or a matron can be more important in making your stay here more comfortable than some of the big bosses in the institution.

13. Many retardates are capable of doing a good job (skilled labor) even though in some ways they are very disturbed.

14. Everyone should have someone in his life whose happiness means as much to him as his own.

15. You should try to be on friendly terms with the attendants and matrons.

16. Retardates should be required to work at a job while here.

TABLE 19 (*continued*)

AGREE

17. Most retardates here are not as stupid as most people think.

18. Everybody has a little bit of something wrong with him.

19. A retardate should try to meet as many other retardates as possible rather than just staying in his own building.

20. Watching television is good for retardates.

DISAGREE

1.* It is important not to think about the life you could lead outside this place as long as you live here.

2. Although retardates may seem all right when they have left here, they should not be allowed to marry.

3. The best way to handle retardates here is to keep them behind locked doors.

4. Regardless of how you look at it, retardates are no longer really human.

5. Once a retardate, always a retardate.

6.* There is little that can be done for a retardate here except to see that he is comfortable and well-fed.

7. An employer would be foolish to hire a retardate who had been here, even if he seems well trained for the job.

8.* It is helpful for retardates to spend most of their time relaxing and enjoying their stay here.

9. It would be hard to develop a close friendship with a person who had been a retardate at this place.

10.* A retardate should try to make his life as simple as possible in this place.

11.* Retardates should spend time getting to know more about themselves by sitting down alone and thinking.

12.* If I had grown up in a normal home, I wouldn't be here.

13.* You have to get to know your matron if you want to get out of this place.

14.* Retardates here should have as much freedom as they want.

15. I don't think there should be places like this, but only places where you don't live in.

16. The law should allow a woman to divorce her husband as soon as he has been in a place like this.

17. The main purpose of a state school for the retarded should be to protect the public from retarded people.

18. Retardates should avoid jobs here because it makes it easier for a person to want to stay here.

19. Every state school for the retarded should be surrounded by a high fence and guards.

20.* A place like this should not ask retardates to do things which they have not done on the outside.

21. As a retardate, one shouldn't spend time getting to know other retardates, especially those who live in other buildings.

22. It would be good for retardates if this place told them what to do all of the time.

23.* Retardates would get better if matrons and attendants did not bother them so much.

24.* Retardates should be permitted to go into town whenever they want to.

25. It is better not to make friends while you are here.

26. It is often better not to have visitors from home because they may upset you.

27. Mental hospitals are better places than state schools.

---

* At least 66 percent of the retardates agree with the item.

"should be allowed to go to town when they wish," but only 16 percent of the Upper and 13 percent of the Lower Staff agree. Moreover, on the item "Retardates should have as much freedom as they want" the divergence is still greater: 4 percent of the Upper Staff and 13 percent of the Lower Staff agree, whereas 87 percent of the retardates agree.

A very striking difference in belief is found when we turn to the etiology of retardation. Given the beliefs held by the experts about retardates, which we described in Chapter 1, it is not surprising that 80 percent of the Upper Staff and 78 percent of the Lower disagree with the statement, "If I had grown up in a normal home, I wouldn't be here." The retardates, not having had the benefit of the experts' opinions, believe that had they been brought up in a normal home they would not be in the training school today (73 percent). On the basis of the data to be presented in the next chapter, it appears that the retardates are quite correct.

TABLE 20

Modal Lower Staff Attitudes

AGREE

---

1. Most retardates in this place are willing to work.

2. When a person has a problem, it is best not to think about it, but keep busy with more pleasant things.

3. Most people are lonely.

4. If you want to get better, it's important to establish a comfortable routine here.

5. You should always do what the matrons and attendants tell you to do, even if you don't want to.

DISAGREE

1.* Retardates here should have something to say about how this place is run.

2.* Retardates should have more say as to whether they should leave or stay here.

3.* The best way to learn about this place is to ask retardates who have been here for some time.

4.* A retardate can't improve unless he is prepared to suffer a little.

---

* At least 66 percent of the retardates agree with the item.

It is, in addition, interesting to note that despite the psychological training of the staff (and in particular the Upper Staff), they are opposed to retardates spending time getting to know more about themselves by sitting alone and thinking (18 percent of Upper and 15 percent of Lower Staff), while an overwhelming majority of retardates (87 percent) want to do just that.

It is apparent, then, that there is a chasm between the world of the retardate and that of the staff. This chasm is, however, further widened when more refined examination of the data is conducted. An additional four attitude items are in conflict between the Lower Staff and the retardates, while 12 more divergent attitudes appear between the Upper Staff and the retardates. (See Tables 20 and 21.)

The conflict between the Lower Staff and the retardates is tempered by at least two factors. First, there are five additional items modal to both groups, indicating a greater similarity in some important aspects of institutional life. For instance, both agree that it is important to establish a comfortable routine, if you want to get better; that it is good to keep busy with pleasant things when you have a problem; and that you should always do what the matrons and attendants tell you to do. Second, many of the items on which the two groups disagree concern management aspects of life in the training school rather than philosophical-theoretical biases. For instance, it is obvious why the Lower Staff do not think that retardates should have a say in the way the training school is run; or why they do not believe that it is good for newcomers to learn about the school from old-timers there (instead, they themselves want to orient and initiate).

In contrast, however, stands the chasm between the retardates and the Upper Staff, predicated not so much by practical, management considerations, but rather by the professionals' almost fervent belief in the "defectiveness" of the youngsters in their care. At first glance the professionals seem to maintain a "humanistic" view of mental retardates which is appropriate to their position and level of education. For example, they dismiss the idea "once a retardate, always a retardate" and feel that "there is nothing wrong with being

TABLE 21

Modal Upper Staff Attitudes

AGREE

---

1. People who were once retardates here are no more dangerous than anyone else.

DISAGREE

1.* In many ways living here is just like living in any other neighborhood you would find.

2.* The best way to fit into this place is to have a good time.

3. All retardates in institutions should be prevented from having children by a painless operation.

4. Being in this place is more helpful to a retardate than being at home or in a foster home.

5. If you want to, it is easy to feel that you are not living in a state school.

6. Even if a retardate who had been here seems better, he should not be given a driver's license.

7.* When a person has a problem, it is best not to think about it, but keep busy with more pleasant things.

8. People who are retarded should never be treated in the same place with other kinds of people.

9.* One of the best spots in this place is the canteen.

10.* A retardate should get to know the people who work here before he starts to get treated for his condition.

11.* A retardate should never leave here unless he is completely well.

12.* The thing most retardates need here is a period of relaxation to get on their feet again.

13.* Most people are lonely.

14.* If I get to live outside, I will try to hide that I was a retardate here.

15.* Everything a retardate does here, including goofing off, helps him get better.

16.* It's kind of easy to fool people who work here.

17.* Most people who work here really don't know what we do at this place.

---

* At least 66 percent of the retardates agree with the item.

retarded." Yet when we look at less transparent statements concerning belief in the inherent and immutable nature of retardation, the professionals are something less than consistent. Thus, one wonders why they disagree that a retardate should not leave the training school unless he is completely well—perhaps, because their "affliction" can never be cured. Or why they think that if retardates had been raised in a normal home, they would still have ended up in a training school—perhaps, because the "affliction" is inherent in the organism. In addition, while most of the retardates (87 percent) feel that the thing they need most is "a period of relaxation to get back on their feet again," and while more than one third of the Lower Staff (38 percent) agree, a mere 6 percent of the Upper Staff are in concordance.

The professional staff also tend to give the retardates less credit for intelligent, manipulative behavior than do the Lower Staff. Only 26 percent of the Upper Staff think that "it is easy for retardates to fool the people who work at the school," 43 percent of the attendants and matrons agree, while 66 percent of the retardates endorsed the statement. Sixty-four percent of the retardates believe that "most people who work here really don't know what we do at this place"; 43 percent of the Lower Staff and just 22 percent of the Upper Staff agree.

As we noted in the last chapter, retardates tend to endorse statements concerning the enjoyment of life while in the training school—for example, "The best way to fit into this place is to have a good time"—a need that would surely be expected of any youngster in a community setting. Eighty-one percent of the retardates responded true to the above statement. Their response found some sympathy among the Lower Staff with 45 percent agreement, but very little among the Upper Staff (22 percent).

Thus another picture begins to emerge when we take the responses of the three main groups together, a picture not of two distinct worlds but of three: the world of the retardate, a very different world of the professional staff, and a third world existing somewhere in between (but closer to the professional world) inhabited by the personnel in closest contact with the retardates, the matrons and attendants.

TABLE 22

*Percent Agreement on RAT Items
for Upper Staff, Lower Staff, and Retardates*

ITEM	UPPER STAFF	LOWER STAFF	RETARDATES	SIGNIFICANT DIFFERENCE BETWEEN
1. More money should be spent by people in the care and treatment of retardates.	92	89	89	
2. Anyone who tries hard to better himself deserves the respect of others.	96	96	86	US–R**; LS–R**
3. If this place had enough well-trained people working here, many of the retardates would improve enough to leave.	76	76	89	US–R**; LS–R**
4. It is better to be a person who is unimportant and honest than to be one who is important and dishonest.	98	96	69	US–R**; LS–R**
5. A person would be foolish not to try to enjoy himself as long as he is in the state school.	70	89	69	US–LS**; LS–R**
6. In many ways living here is just like living in any other neighborhood you would find.	18	33	64	US–R**; LS–R**

7. The head of this school should try hard to get attendants who are able to get along with the retardates.	96	89	93	
8. The best way to handle people is to tell them what they want to hear.	12	22	89	US–R**; LS–R**
9. It is important not to think about the life you could lead outside this place as long as you live here.	8	29	62	US–LS**; US–R**; LS–R**
10. More than anything else, the retardates need the respect and understanding of the people who work with them.	100	98	94	US–R**
11. The best things this school can do for a retardate cannot help him unless he also tries to help himself.	82	83	89	
12. The best way to fit into this place is to have a good time.	22	45	81	US–LS**; US–R**; LS–R**
13. If you really want to, it is not too hard to leave this place.	35	57	66	US–LS**; US–R**
14. It is possible to have a good life here.	80	93	62	US–R**; LS–R**
15. Although retardates may seem all right when they have left here, they should not be allowed to marry.	27	26	34	

TABLE 22 (cont'd)

ITEM	UPPER STAFF	LOWER STAFF	RETARDATES	SIGNIFICANT DIFFERENCE BETWEEN
16. The best way to handle retardates here is to keep them behind locked doors.	0	2	19	US–R**; LS–R**
17. A person can be good in every way.	24	39	84	US–R**; LS–R**
18. Regardless of how you look at it, retardates are no longer really human.	2	0	32	US–R**; LS–R**
19. Once a retardate, always a retardate.	12	24	40	US–R**; LS–R**
20. It's important for a retardate to have a sense of humor.	72	80	79	
21. Never tell anyone the real reason you did something unless it will be helpful to you.	4	25	70	US–LS**; US–R**; LS–R**
22. There is nothing wrong with being retarded.	92	78	66	US–R**
23. There is little that can be done for a retardate here except to see that he is comfortable and well-fed.	0	7	82	US–R**; LS–R**
24. Anyone who completely trusts anyone else is asking for trouble.	16	27	47	US–R**; LS–R**
25. All retardates in institutions should be prevented from having children by a painless operation.	24	44	47	US–LS*; US–R**

26. An employer would be foolish to hire a retardate who had been here, even if he seems well trained for the job.	0	2	49	US–R**; LS–R**
27. There are many people on the outside more disturbed than retardates who have been here for a long time.	93	93	77	US–R**; LS–R**
28. Most people won't work hard at things unless they are forced to.	26	33	67	US–R**; LS–R**
29. It is helpful for retardates to spend most of their time relaxing and enjoying their stay here.	20	26	69	US–R**; LS–R**
30. Being in this place is more helpful to a retardate than being at home or in a foster home.	20	43	53	US–LS**; US–R**
31. It is a good thing to treat retardates with kindness but it will probably not help them get any smarter.	47	54	69	US–R**; LS–R**
32. It would be hard to develop a close friendship with a person who had been a retardate at this place.	16	15	53	US–R**; LS–R**
33. People who were once retardates here are no more dangerous than anyone else.	90	61	68	US–LS**; US–R**
34. People should be sure they are doing the right thing before they do it.	78	89	85	

TABLE 22 (cont'd)

ITEM	UPPER STAFF	LOWER STAFF	RETARDATES	SIGNIFICANT DIFFERENCE BETWEEN
35. A retardate should try to make his life as simple as possible in this place.	14	28	83	US–R**; LS–R**
36. Retardates should spend time getting to know more about themselves by sitting down alone and thinking.	18	15	87	US–R**; LS–R**
37. If you want to, it is easy to feel that you are not living in a state school.	10	40	58	US–LS*; US–R**; LS–R**
38. Most retardates in this place are willing to work.	66	78	93	US–R**; LS–R**
39. If I had grown up in a normal home, I wouldn't be here.	20	22	73	US–R**; LS–R**
40. Retardates here should have something to say about how this place is run.	37	24	77	US–R**; LS–R**
41. You have to get to know your matron if you want to get out of this place.	30	26	88	US–R**; LS–R**
42. The best way to get help for your problems is to keep busy and forget you are a retardate.	36	59	83	US–LS**; US–R**; LS–R**
43. Retardates here should have as much freedom as they want.	4	15	87	US–R**; LS–R**

44. Even if a retardate who had been here seems better, he should not be given a driver's license.	20	45	40	US–LS**; US–R**
45. It is important to learn all about this place if you want to get things done and enjoy yourself.	50	61	87	US–R**; LS–R**
46. I don't think there should be places like this, but only places where you don't live in.	6	13	55	US–R**; LS–R**
47. Sometimes an attendant or a matron can be more important in making your stay here more comfortable than some of the big bosses in the institution.	96	100	78	US–R**; LS–R**
48. Many retardates are capable of doing a good job (skilled labor) even though in some ways they are very disturbed.	84	98	85	US–LS**; LS–R**
49. The saying that there is a sucker born every minute is right.	30	54	71	US–LS**; US–R**; LS–R**
50. When a person has a problem, it is best not to think about it, but keep busy with more pleasant things.	26	74	86	US–LS**; US–R**; LS–R**
51. People who are retarded should never be treated in the same place with other kinds of people.	10	33	51	US–LS**; US–R**; LS–R**

TABLE 22 (cont'd)

ITEM	UPPER STAFF	LOWER STAFF	RETARDATES	SIGNIFICANT DIFFERENCE BETWEEN
52. The only hope for a retardate here is to get understanding.	36	57	71	US–LS*; US–R**; LS–R**
53. Anyone who is in an institution for the retarded should not be allowed to vote.	40	41	35	
54. The law should allow a woman to divorce her husband as soon as he has been in a place like this.	16	24	40	US–R**; LS–R**
55. A retardate should not think about leaving here but rather how he can get better.	39	61	73	US–LS**; US–R**
56. The main purpose of a state school for the retarded should be to protect the public from retarded people.	2	11	58	US–R**; LS–R**
57. Everyone should have someone in his life whose happiness means as much to him as his own.	90	100	86	US–LS**; LS–R**
58. Retardates should avoid jobs here because jobs make it easier for a person to want to stay here.	4	17	50	US–LS*; US–R**; LS–R**

59. One of the best spots in this place is the canteen.	24	33	84	US–R**; LS–R**
60. I know of retardates who are really well enough to leave, but they enjoy it here and want to stay.	64	63	56	
61. A retardate should get to know the people who work here before he starts to get treated for his condition.	20	40	76	US–LS*; US–R**; LS–R**
62. Most people who get ahead in the world lead good clean lives.	30	37	86	US–R**; LS–R**
63. A retardate should never leave here unless he is completely well.	16	43	76	US–LS**; US–R**; LS–R**
64. A woman would be foolish to marry a retardate.	44	57	37	LS–R**
65. Every state school for the retarded should be surrounded by a high fence and guards.	2	2	27	US–R**; LS–R**
66. The thing most retardates need here is a period of relaxation to get on their feet again.	6	38	87	US–LS**; US–R**; LS–R**
67. A person who has been in a state school should not be allowed to be a mayor.	60	58	35	US–R**; LS–R**
68. Most people are lonely.	30	77	79	US–LS**; US–R**
69. If you want to get better, it's important to establish a comfortable routine here.	56	84	82	US–LS**; US–R**

TABLE 22 (cont'd)

ITEM	UPPER STAFF	LOWER STAFF	RETARDATES	SIGNIFICANT DIFFERENCE BETWEEN
70. Retardates should have more say as to whether they should leave or stay here.	40	18	76	US–LS**; US–R**; LS–R**
71. A place like this should not ask retardates to do things which they have not done on the outside.	4	18	68	US–LS**; US–R**; LS–R**
72. As a retardate, one shouldn't spend time getting to know other retardates, especially those who live in other buildings.	4	25	61	US–LS**; US–R**; LS–R**
73. If I get to live outside, I will try to hide that I was a retardate here.	26	31	66	US–R**; LS–R**
74. The best way to learn about this place is to ask retardates who have been here for some time.	36	22	85	US–R**; LS–R**
75. Most men are brave.	40	43	88	US–R**; LS–R**
76. A retardate can't improve unless he is prepared to suffer a little.	36	26	67	US–R**; LS–R**
77. Retardates here would feel better if this place did not bother them.	42	67	82	US–LS**; US–R**; LS–R**
78. You should try to be on friendly terms with the attendants and matrons.	92	91	76	US–R**; LS–R**

79. Everything a retardate does here, including goofing off, helps him get better.	12	39	63	US–LS**; US–R**; LS–R**
80. Retardates should be required to work at a job while here.	86	83	91	
81. It would be good for retardates if this place told them what to do all of the time.	12	2	44	US–R**; LS–R**
82. Most retardates here are not as stupid as most people think.	80	93	82	LS–R**
83. Retardates would get better if matrons and attendants did not bother them so much.	26	22	80	US–R**; LS–R**
84. Everybody has a little bit of something wrong with them.	94	93	89	
85. You can be sure that most people have a mean streak and they will show it whenever they have the chance.	14	57	88	US–LS**; US–R**; LS–R**
86. Retardates should be permitted to go into town whenever they want to.	16	13	71	US–R**; LS–R**
87. It's a smart thing to be nice to important people.	54	54	93	US–R**; LS–R**
88. A retardate should try to meet as many other retardates as possible rather than just staying in his own building.	94	89	82	US–R**
89. It is better not to make friends while you are here.	6	4	33	US–R**; LS–R**

TABLE 22 (cont'd)

ITEM	UPPER STAFF	LOWER STAFF	RETARDATES	SIGNIFICANT DIFFERENCE BETWEEN
90. Honesty is always the best policy.	82	87	87	
91. You should always do what matrons and attendants tell you to do, even if you don't want to.	50	60	96	US–R**; LS–R**
92. Most people are good and kind.	68	74	92	US–R**; LS–R**
93. There are good reasons for lying sometimes.	68	63	60	
94. Watching television is good for retardates.	82	91	84	
95. Retardates always come to this place because they are forced to by others.	60	39	55	US–LS*; LS–R**
96. It is often better not to have visitors from home because they may upset you.	8	24	38	US–LS*; US–R**; LS–R**
97. It is hard to get ahead without cheating.	4	13	69	US–R**; LS–R**
98. Mental hospitals are better places than state schools.	10	11	47	US–R**; LS–R**
99. It's kind of easy to fool people who work here.	26	43	66	US–R**; LS–R**
100. Most people who work here really don't know what we do at this place.	22	43	64	US–LS***; US–R**; LS–R**

* $p < .025$
** $p < .01$

Stylistic similarities in problem-solving strategies also may be found between the retardates and the Lower Staff, in sharp contradiction to the professional group: 74 percent of the Lower Staff, 86 percent of the retardates, and only 26 percent of the Upper Staff agree that "when a person has a problem, it is best not to think about it, but keep busy with more pleasant things." The most striking difference between the three groups is, perhaps, summed up by their responses to the item "Most people are lonely"—79 percent of the retardates, 77 percent of the Lower Staff, and 30 percent of the Upper Staff agree.

Additional evidence for the three worlds can be found in our analysis of the differences between percentages obtained by the three groups on each item. This analysis is more refined than the preceding since it differentiates between the magnitude of concordance. Thus, although an item may be modal (70 percent or more concordance) for two groups, there may be a large difference between them in magnitude (for example, 71 percent versus 98 percent). This analysis reveals that the retardates and Upper Staff are significantly different ($p < .025$) on 80 of the 100 items; the retardates and Lower Staff on 76 of the items; and the Upper Staff and Lower Staff on one third (33) of the items (see Table 22).

These differences in world view may be explained and interpreted in a variety of ways (for example, differences in social class, education, ethnic background, or intelligence). The point we are making here is that regardless of the reasons, the retardate is faced with living in the institution the way he personally desires while confronted with the frequently conflicting desires of the professionals and subprofessionals. The impact of our earlier findings, therefore, takes on greater in concordance with the retardates about how they should live and what is "good" for them, then the presence of different styles of adaptation could be viewed as a function of the strength in the light of this conflict. That is, if the staff were staff's influence. The results of this chapter make it clear that the personal styles of adaptation the retardates evolve are hard-won victories, requiring the weapons of cleverness, resourcefulness, and interpersonal skill. Perhaps the one thing retardates have "going for them" is that the staff, especially the professionals, cannot imagine that these "defective" creatures have the intelligence, manipulativeness, and other skills necessary to regulate one's life in an institutional setting. The retardates can, therefore, exercise their abilities without detection—in short, the staff does not know what is happening. Again, it should be stressed that the professionals are the ones who are most ignorant of the retardates' behavior. They have the lowest expectations of them and the greatest social distance from them. The Lower Staff, on the other hand, have learned to some extent what these youngsters are capable of, or perhaps have never had the professional training to blind them from the context in which the retardates' behavior occurs and the intentionality of their behavior. For example, when we were selecting retardates to serve as subjects in our studies, it was the matrons and attendants who told us who were the really "smart" ones (even though their IQ's were below our criteria), the ones who could handle themselves in an interview, understand instructions, and so on, despite the diagnostic categories to which the professionals assigned them.

The question that next comes to mind is: If these youngsters are so clever, manipulative, and resourceful, what are they doing in a training school for the mentally retarded? How did they ever get diagnosed or labeled "retarded"? And why was it deemed necessary to incarcerate them?

These questions are at first puzzling. Could all the persons involved in the institutionalization of a single child—the social workers, teachers, psychologists, psychiatrists, the parents— could they all be wrong? The following chapters are addressed to this troubling notion. Specifically, we will examine exactly how the retardates became labeled retarded and consequently institutionalized.

CHAPTER

6

The Children's Heritage

An excursion into the bleak past of the youngsters we studied provides ample information about why they have been institutionalized, albeit for reasons other than mental retardation. Although the histories and recollections will be limited, to some extent, by the perspective of the informant, they may, nonetheless, enable us to gain important insights into the process of incarceration. To overcome the problem of personal or professional biases, the material we will present here represents the polarities in perspectives concerning retardation—the social workers and the retardates—making any concurrence in the histories all the more meaningful.

First, let us see what the retardates have to say. In our interviews (described in Chapter 4) all the retardates were asked: "Why are you here at the training school?" Since, as we noted earlier, 93 percent of the retardates did not believe that they were retarded, their responses to this question were varied and personal. Some representative answers are presented below.

WHY ARE YOU HERE?

Mr. K. W.   AGE: *20 yrs.*   AGE AT ADMISSION: *10 yrs.*

Busted up, that's why I came here. A lot of them come here from broken homes—the parents got divorced or maybe some-one passed away in the family or one reason or another. Well, for instance, like when I came here I wasn't retarded and I'm not a retardate. I came here from a broken home. My father was a little ill and he had something wrong. They gave him a helping hand to get him on the right track. So in the meantime my mother was on welfare. She didn't use it right, so they put the kids away. If I could have done something about it I would have because I feel the training school should be strictly mental retardates. There's a lot of others like myself that are here that are not mentally retarded or anything. They should not have been here either. They should be in a foster home or a school.

Mr. D. P.   AGE: *14 yrs.*   AGE AT ADMISSION: *9 yrs.*

I hate to mention it. . . . I was living with my real mother and she died and so my father came home from the service and picked me up and my father found another woman so he married her and I'm his son and my brother's stepbrother. . . . My stepmother ain't so good to me. See my father wants me out, but my mother wants me here. My stepmother, she wants me here, my father wants me out. So I don't know which it's going to be.

Mr. R. P.   AGE: *13 yrs.*   AGE AT ADMISSION: *5 yrs.*

Because my father he was working. My father had a divorce in 1958 and after that he had a job. He was working on radios and stuff. He had no money or nothing and he can't support me or nothing, so he put me here. . . . My father is going to take me out in June for good.

Mr. P. G.   AGE: *14 yrs.*   AGE AT ADMISSION: *6 yrs.*

I don't know. I came here when I was six years old and I am still here now. . . . I want to get out of here. . . . I don't even remember what happened before I came here. My parents sent the whole family somewhere. I got a sister that's in a foster home. I got a brother who was in here. He went to a foster home. And I got another brother in N.L. . . . I seen them [parents] last Christmas. That's the first time I seen my mother in seven years.

Mr. I. D.   AGE: *20 yrs.*   AGE AT ADMISSION: *15 yrs.*

Oh, I had trouble in school and I had broken into stores. . . . I'd rather be on the outside working than being cooped up in this joint. . . . I'm homesick. I've been here almost five years. I have suffered anger from being here. I can't sleep at night. I cry in my sleep. I get very nervous. I take off from here every six months. I run home to my parents. The last time I was home Christmas time I told my mother I will come home and go away—permanently! I will get married, change my name, grow a beard and mustache, if I have to, and I will leave [this state] behind.

Mr. W. F.   AGE: *14 yrs.*   AGE AT ADMISSION: *9 yrs.*

Because I got in a lot of trouble on the outside . . . playing hooky. . . . I got a mother but I ain't got a father. The social

worker sent me here. . . . I'm not retarded. I'm smart. I d
go to school. I'm in the eighth grade. This place is for re
tardates—yeah, and for kids who do bad things on the outsid
too.

Mr. C. W.   AGE: *14 yrs.*   AGE AT ADMISSION: *9 yrs*

I don't know . . . when I was at school I got into trouble . .
you know, laying down in the street, me and my other friends
fooling around in the street . . . figured it out for myself, n
one told me why. . . . This place is for the mentally retarde
kids and all that . . . or somebody that, you know, they throv
them up here. They ain't got no other place to put them lik
[a children's home] or something like that. Might as well throv
them up here.

Mr. B. R.   AGE: *19 yrs.*   AGE AT ADMISSION: *12 yrs*

I'd been stealing—been stealing—breaking into houses an
stuff like that. . . . I had a choice. I could go to [a reformatory
for boys] or go here. That's even worse down there. . . . Ther
is some of them boys here that have rich parents. They sen
them here to keep them out of their purse.

Mr. M. C.   AGE: *20 yrs.*   AGE AT ADMISSION: *9 yrs*

My mother told me I wasn't put here as mental retardation
I was put in here because I was a juvenile delinquent when
was small. . . . I don't think I'd even be here. My mother, sh
didn't really put me here, but at the time she didn't have n
way of taking care of me either. So this is where she stuck me

Miss W. E.   AGE: *23 yrs.*   AGE AT ADMISSION: *16 yrs*

That's a good question. I don't know. . . . Well, I thought a
first I was put here for school and to learn how to work. But

ee whiz, I've been out of school for three years now and I've
een working in the infirmary and I should know how to work
y now. . . . I don't like to talk about it . . . something I did
n the outside. It was a mistake. Everybody makes mistakes
. . that's why I think I'm here. My mother and father never
old me why, but I guessed it. When I was sixteen it happened.

---

liss K. G.　　　　AGE: *19 yrs.*　　　　AGE AT ADMISSION: *14 yrs.*

ecause I've been separated and I had so many homes that
 had moved to—so they figured I should come here. It's too
lany homes. Too many. Separated from my own sister. I was
n a foster home with my sister. She's working in [a mental
ospital] now. She works on one of the wards up there. . . .
he social workers, they don't really tell you why, they just put
ou here. I came to court and the court told me to come here,
oo. The man took me there, my social worker. If I didn't have
his place I'd be wandering from place to place. . . .

---

liss J. N.　　　　AGE: *30 yrs.*　　　　AGE AT ADMISSION: *9 yrs.*

ecause my family put me here—because I needed schooling
nd I didn't have enough training. . . . I came here when I
vas nine . . . because I had been in a lot of accidents, car
ccidents. I don't like cars. . . . It's better being in [the train-
ng school] than being on the streets. There are places like in
Korea or Vietnam where there are no places to live. I feel
orry for them.

---

liss C. R.　　　　AGE: *24 yrs.*　　　　AGE AT ADMISSION: *12 yrs.*

'm here to learn and to get along with people and to try to go
ut in the community and to try to do the best that I can.
. . I was put out in the street when I was nine and there was
o one to take care of me.

Miss K. B.　　AGE: *27 yrs.*　　AGE AT ADMISSION: *15 yr*

I hated school. I used to skip out a lot. . . . I've been here ı
years the 21st of October . . . just after my father died.

Miss C. R.　　AGE: *21 yrs.*　　AGE AT (MOST RECENT
ADMISSION: *16 yı*

I'm not telling you. It's my personal business . . . the first tin
I came in because of a broken home. My mother and father g￼
divorced. I don't bother my real mother. I live with my fost￼
mother now. My real mother sent me here (when I was thi
teen) because I never really got along with her. . . . I had ￼
come in. The social worker took me out of school. . . . I wer
on parole at fifteen—how is anyone supposed to know an
thing at fifteen? I went to [a large city] and after, I got in￼
trouble. I got in with the wrong crowd. I was living in [a ha￼
way house]—they find you a job and you pay them boar￼
. . . I took off from the [half-way house], another girl and ￼
. . . they were looking for us. We got in with some boys, an
that's all. So I was in the sheriff's office—the police statio￼
They called up the training school. So, I got back.

Miss R. C.　　AGE: *28 yrs.*　　AGE AT ADMISSION: *12 yr*

I think I did something wrong. I was twelve.

Miss J. P.　　AGE: *16 yrs.*　　AGE AT ADMISSION: *14 yr*

Well this is a long story but—well this happened in a hom￼
when I was home. My brother—I had trouble with my brothe
Well, he got me pregnant. I was living with a foster moth￼
and my brother, he was a stepbrother. He's seventeen. We￼
I had the baby and the baby passed—the baby died. And I wa
so unhappy. I thought the baby would live, but it didn't. M
[foster] mother was glad the baby died, but I wasn't glad. An￼

he blamed me and I blamed her and I got all mixed up. She blamed me for everything. When I came here she told the charge aide—she said she didn't blame me. She thought it was my [real] mother's fault. . . . I have a father, but I don't know where he is. I guess he lives with my sister. My mother died when I was twelve years old. She died of a heart attack. . . . I was thirteen or fourteen when I had the baby . . . a lot of girls come here because they are having childs. Some girls I know had babies already.

Miss T. D.	AGE: *15 yrs.*	AGE AT ADMISSION: *3 yrs.*

don't know. I was a baby and they brought me in a carriage.

The picture of the past that the retardates described is replete with illness, poverty, family disintegration, delinquency, sexual misconduct, and personal betrayal. The descriptions offered by the social case workers, although more detailed, contain substantially the same elements as the retardates' portrayal. The case records that follow, altered only when anonymity would be violated, are typical of the 177 retardate histories that we examined.

SOCIAL CASEWORKER RECORDS

Case 1	*Miss R. O.*	AGE AT ADMISSION: 15

Paternal mother showed little interest in R. O. and placed her in the home of a friend when she was one year old. At this time the mother was behaving promiscuously and in a generally socially unacceptable manner. She was arrested several times for nonsupport of the child, intoxication, theft, and breach of peace. Mother has had no contact with the child since one year of age and her whereabouts are unknown. . . . The child was born after her parents separated and the father denied paternity of the child. The child was in one loving foster home

until she was three years of age, but foster parents were i
and could not take care of her. In the second foster home sh
was never completely accepted. Foster mother is threatened b
any behavior which is not completely acceptable. The foste
mother has requested R. C.'s immediate removal. She ha
stated that she does not intend to enroll the child in school.

Case 2   *Mr. D. X.*   AGE AT ADMISSION:

Father is at present a prisoner. Father had a fifth-grade educa
tion and he and 22 other siblings had been wards of the state
D. X.'s mother had 14 siblings. Father is indifferent to all 1
children. Mother is promiscuous and married illegally becaus
father is still married to first wife. The children were born ou
of wedlock. Father supports family on disability pension an
erratic wages. The neighbors complain about them. Police in
vestigated and caught father in act of having sexual relation
with the seven-year-old daughter. Two brothers also joined i
this activity for several years. Father imprisoned for inces
Family lacks food, clothing, and heat. Children removed from
home and hospitalized because of incest.

Case 3   *Mr. J. L.*   AGE AT ADMISSION:

J. L. is an illegitimate child. He lives with his grandmothe
maternal aunt, aunt's child, and the child of an institutionalize
maternal aunt. Mother is considered limited . . . at age c
three she was admitted to a training school for three years
When I arrived for a scheduled visit recently I found th
mother holding J. L., her son, by a rope tied around his wais
. . . Mother has consistently asked for J. L.'s removal as a
unmanageable child. . . . J. L. has appeared at school with rop
marks on his neck and back. He has been seen running wildl
about the house with three adults chasing him. . . . J. L. is
stocky, somewhat obese boy. . . . He is a behavior problem
destructive and unmanageable both at home and the com

1unity. His mother is unable to give him the necessary struc-
1red environment and education. . . . J. L. verbalizes a strong
sentment against his mother whom he claims beats him. He
sked to live away from his mother.

ase 4   **Mr. R. B.**   AGE AT ADMISSION: *11*

'ather had been in prison because of sexual relations with his
aughter, and has had a grammar school education. R. B. has
1e emotionally disturbed brother and two retarded brothers.
Ine sister is disturbed, delinquent, promiscuous, and had
exual relations with father. Other sister has emotional prob-
ems, delinquent, promiscuous, and also had sexual relations
vith father. The sisters were felt to have seduced the father.
. B.'s mother died and was alcoholic, disturbed mentally and
motionally, neglectful of children. After mother's death all
1e children were taken by the DCG. After second marriage
1e children lived with father and stepmother. Stepmother is
imited and considered retarded. Stepmother is anxious to place
hildren . . . is unable and unwilling to care for them. She is
ostile towards them, possibly caused by feeling the daughters
educed her husband. Advised to admit R. B. because of re-
ardation and poor home environment. Has been neglected
hysically and emotionally. Father has evaded responsibility
s provider and is also abusive.

ase 5   **Mr. S. D.**   AGE AT ADMISSION: 5

. D. is an illegitimate child. The father is unknown. Step-
1ther is an immigrant in the U.S. for several years. The mother
f S. D. had a stormy childhood. Was the ward of the state for
ears. Through the ages of four until eight she was placed in
ve different homes. She has a seventh-grade education. S. D.
vas sired by a displaced person who refused to marry. He was
laced in a foster home at three months old—was there until
1ree and a half years of age. Mother felt S. D. was a spoiled

child and that he could be a good child if he could be take
care of properly. Mother and child appear to need help des
perately. Actually separation of the child from his mother ma
make him more disturbed; but I see little chance at mothe
being able to cope with this child. S. D. doesn't get along wit
others, wets the bed, nervous and sucks fingers; child under
stands Russian better than English.

Case 6   *Miss P. F.*   AGE AT ADMISSION:

Father is a sailor. Parents are separated. The children fear th
father who drinks, beats mother, and is sexually demanding
Mother spends money on herself rather than on childre
. . . No evidence of maternal feeling and no significant rela
tionships with her children. Mother has had four suicid
attempts and diagnosed as psychopath with antisocial tender
cies. Miss P. F. appeared to be physically and emotionall
starved. She has witnessed father's sexual attacks on th
mother. This made her upset and she has tried to imitate i
P. F. is active and high-strung. She learned nothing in kinder
garten.

Case 7   *Mr. R. Z.*   AGE AT ADMISSION:

Father is a laborer. Mother had a very limited and impover
ished childhood. Mother had incestuous relations with ma
ternal grandfather and was promiscuous with numerous men
She was committed to prison for two years. R. Z. at the age o
four and his six siblings became wards of the state. He was sen
to four foster homes before admission here. Foster parent
don't seem to be able to give R. Z. the intensive supervision h
requires. All the children are either in institutions for th
retarded or in prison. R. Z. seemingly cannot control destruc
tiveness. In addition, he presents a hazard since his learning o
the use of matches and his progressive fondness to set fires. H
is extremely stubborn and overly slow in school.

Case 8 | *Miss G. F.* | AGE AT ADMISSION: 7

Her father deserted family when she was four months old. He was reported to have attempted perverse sex actions with a child. Mother divorced from father, married and divorced again. She is said to have limited mental capacity, low social standing, and hated her children. Mother is now living with an unmarried man and has had two children by him. . . . G. F. at four months of age was placed with maternal uncle and aunt for three years. She was discovered at three years of age, filthy, emaciated, weighing fourteen pounds. She was then kept by Mrs. X until she was five years of age and then went to live with her paternal grandmother until she was six and a half years of age. She was referred to the Childrens Service Bureau by two aunts. In school she was inattentive and hyperactive.

Case 9 | *Mr. J. L.* | AGE AT ADMISSION: 10

Reason for admission is unsuccessful foster home placement. J. L. and eight sibs had been taken over by child welfare because of living in a shack under dreadful conditions. Father has seventh-grade education, no occupation, and has arthritis and limited intelligence. Mother has sixth-grade education. She is divorced from first husband. J. L. spent two years in grade one and one year each in grades two and three. Report of teacher at school is that J. L.'s behavior is satisfactory. His speech is improved. When found in shack with mother, J. L. could only make guttural sounds. Comprehension is good, but manual dexterity is poor. The reason for his admission, then, is poor adjustment in several foster homes even though the homes were good.

Case 10 | *Mr. M. R.* | AGE AT ADMISSION: 9

One of four children. Mother deserted children. Father is in prison for neglect of children. Mother has court record for truancy and delinquency. She is in jail for neglect of children and for adultery. M. R. has been placed in seven foster homes. In school he attended kindergarten at six years, spent one year in first grade and was repeating second grade when he was excluded because of soiling and wetting his clothing while in school. He is described as a restless, insecure, rather sly and sneaky little boy who does not like to mind and is somewhat abusive to those younger than himself. Application for admission by Department of Child Guidance.

Case 11   *Mr. J. V.*   AGE AT ADMISSION: 7

J. V. is an illegitimate child. Father is unknown and reported to be a drug addict who worked as a carnival pitchman. Mother has a high-school education. She has been married once, had one son, then divorced and remarried, and then divorced again. She became pregnant from "carnival man," but he was so brutal she wouldn't marry him. She is in poor health and unemployed. Her parents send her money. She has no maternal feelings for her two children. She maintained she couldn't care for him even as a baby and wished for adoption. J. V. has trouble completing a given task and has a very short attention span. He works well in arts and crafts.

Case 12   *Mr. K. L.*   AGE AT ADMISSION: 7

K. L. lives with father and stepmother. Father has a seventh-grade education. K. L.'s mother died three days after his birth. She was known to have run around and drank heavily. She was an illegitimate child. Father's family are degenerate and of low mentality. He was committed at one time to a county temporary home. He married and was divorced on charges of cruelty and abusive treatment. He married K. L.'s mother. She died and he remarried. The stepmother is a withdrawn person. After K. L.'s mother's death, father placed K. L. with maternal great-aunt, then father had child boarded in several homes. When he remarried, the wife would take K. L. only if she had guardianship. Father was unwilling to give him up to an unwilling stepmother. He committed the child to a foster home and the child was placed back home with the father after stepmother had a child. K. L. is affectionate when alone with a person who accepts his affection. Otherwise, he is a whipped puppy dog.

Case 13   **Mr. P. C.**   AGE AT ADMISSION: 5

Mother had a third-grade education and father is a college graduate. Mother appears to be of low intelligence. She does not feel able to take care of the child. I have been unable to contact mother except by a few phone calls. The father has been drifting from job to job. Father is considered to be mentally disturbed. He had been discharged or quit many jobs because he is unable to get along with superiors. He is intellectually a bright person who uses big and uncommon words. The family life is a turbulent situation. Parents have separated several times. The father blames his wife for the child's condition. He said he had the misfortune to marry a mentally deficient woman. P. C. has been referred because of the poor adjustment he is making in the home of his grandparents following his parents' separation. The divorce case is pending. P. C. has the distressing habit of banging his head. The mother slept late so to get attention he would bang his head on the crib. He has poor reality testing but not necessarily due to retardation but to life experiences.

Case 14   **Mr. W. K.**   AGE AT ADMISSION: 9

Father has a third-grade education. Mother has none. Father is an alcoholic and has been arrested by police for drunkenness and neglect. Received a six-month sentence for nonsupport. He is in jail now and is divorced. Family is on welfare. Petitions of neglect have been filed. The children are neglected and uncared for. The family has long been a problem to the community. The impression of the school and housing authorities is that the mother is incapable of providing a suitable parent-child relationship. She is very limited intellectually. Has been arrested and convicted of lascivious carriage. She has been evicted by housing authorities because of immoral purposes. W. K. and three sibs were sent to the institution after coming in contact with the police for delinquent behavior.

Case 15   *Mr. C. B.*   AGE AT ADMISSION: 9

Father and mother have grammar school education. Father is an alcoholic and abused mother and children. Mother is divorced from second husband and is planning to get married again. There is a lot of dissension in the home. She is employed as a maid at a hotel. Mother does seem to reject the boy. She appears to be a rather dull person herself, and police feel that some of her objections are on the basis that she intends to remarry and does not want C. B. C. B.'s father was abusive and strapped him to chairs and refused to let him play. C. B. was picked up by police for throwing rocks at a dilapidated 1939 Chevrolet on a vacant lot. Mother told police her son even breaks his own toys and is destructive.

Case 16   *Miss Z. L.*   AGE AT ADMISSION: 6

Miss Z. L. has no known father. She had been admitted to the Department of Child Guidance as neglected when three years old. She has never attended school. She is suggestible, cries when teased, seclusive and emotionally unstable, and is easily upset. Reported to be resentful of authority, resents help of any kind, independent and somewhat stubborn, and is vain. DCG found her suffering from malnutrition. One sister was sent to the state mental hospital when she was eight years of age.

Case 17   *Miss B. L.*   AGE AT ADMISSION: 7

Miss B. L. has never attended school. She was committed to DCG when one year old . . . has been in many foster homes.

Her father has been arrested many times for nonsupport and died at the age of twenty-five. Her mother died of cancer. Miss B. L. has two sisters here (training school). The oldest brother cared for her and sibs. The SPCC testified that the beds were verminous, house filthy, with the mother and four children sharing one bed. The father alleged to have attempted incest with his oldest daughter. Brother served time for drunkenness and nonsupport of his children.

Case 18   *Miss P. K.*   AGE AT ADMISSION: 5

Father's occupation not determined. Parents are separated. P. K. lived at home until she was four. Father deserted as there were too many children in the house. Is now living with another woman. P. K. was placed in children's welfare house when four and then placed in foster home. She had good care but is too difficult to handle. Is said to be quarrelsome and once threw a knife at foster mother.

Case 19   *Miss K. N.*   AGE AT ADMISSION: 9

Sent here by orphanage. Father was fifty-nine years old when K. N. was born. Mother forty-two years old. Father has seventh-grade education and mother completed six years of schooling. Mother appears mentally disturbed. K. N. was placed in orphanage as a neglected child. She was found eating uncooked meat and no vegetables. The Sisters described her as a little animal when the child came to the orphanage. She has improved at the orphanage.

Case 20   *Miss L. O.*   AGE AT ADMISSION: 7

Father wants child committed because unable to do first-grade work. Father is said to be alcoholic, lazy, and neglectful of family. He works occasionally. The family is often on welfare.

The home is a small shack in poor condition. The mother has IQ of 60 and is said to be inadequate and neglectful of family.

Our subjects, to say the least, did not come from ideal or even average milieus. Most of their homes (64 percent) were characterized by the absence of one parent as a result of desertion, divorce, separation, imprisonment, or some other form of institutionalization. Those who had both parents at home (36 percent) at the time of their incarceration as retardates were not, however, guaranteed better home lives. To the contrary, 59 percent of the youngsters in this group come from families characterized as having a "bad influence" (incest, beatings, starvation, and so on) on the children's development.

In addition to the familial disruption, "unwholesomeness" and marginality of the families, their backgrounds include extreme economic and educational impoverishment. More than half of the families of our subjects (51 percent) were receiving some form of public support. The parents who were employed, however, offered their families little more financially than those on welfare. Most (48 percent) worked at very low-salaried menial jobs, 29 percent at semiskilled jobs, 19 percent at skilled work, and only 4 percent as clerks or at other minor white-collar jobs. The formal educational levels attained by the parents parallel their employment levels. A mere 4 percent had some college education, 22 percent graduated from high school, 26 percent had some high school, and 48 percent had a grammar school education or less.

The economic, educational, and familial marginality represents only part of the backgrounds of the children we studied. A child can, no doubt, come from a poor, fragmented family yet still grow up to become an outstanding member of the community. The kind of home life the child experiences, the "influence" the family exerts on the child, is, perhaps, more crucial to his development than his family's statistical placement on various dimensions. It is no surprise, then, that 63 percent of our subjects' families were reported by observers as being "bad influences" on the children. This does not imply that the remaining 37 percent of the families were "good influences"

—their records simply did not have any information at all concerning the treatment and care of the children.

The preinstitutional lives of our subjects and the characteristics of their families are in no way unusual. The centuries-old notion that the preponderance of the "stupid," "defective," "dangerous," and "insane" come from the lower class, the disreputable poor, has been corroborated by recent findings. Benda, Squires, Ogonik, and Wise (1963) found that of the 205 slightly retarded children they studied, only one third came from intact families; only one fourth of the homes could provide subsistence levels of food, clothing and shelter; less than 1 percent of the families had no contact with public welfare agencies; and so on. Farber (1968), after reviewing the literature in this area, summarizes the findings in the following statement:

> Families of educable retardates display environments that are unstable and stultifying. These families show much instability through divorce and desertion, a high degree of contact with social welfare agencies, and a large number of police arrests. Moreover, when lower-class families are considered, those with a mildly retarded child reveal a low degree of participation in voluntary associations, a tendency to belong to isolated religious sects rather than to major denominations, infrequent church attendance, relatively little contact with friends and neighbors, and a high residential mobility. There tends to be a low level of education of the parents, low income per family member, poor health, and little exposure to mass communication media such as movies, magazines, and newspapers. The home tends to be overcrowded [pp. 174–175].

The miserable backgrounds of these children, then, have not gone unnoticed. The President's Panel on Mental Retardation (1962), despite other oversights, focuses clearly on the link between human squalor and misery, and intrapsychic "defects."

> The majority of the mentally retarded are the children of the more disadvantaged classes of our society. This extraordinarily heavy prevalence in certain deprived population groups suggests a major causative role, in some way not yet fully delineated, for

adverse social, economic, and cultural factors. These conditions may not only mean absence of the physical necessities of life, but the lack of opportunity and motivation . . . the correction of these fundamental conditions is necessary to prevent mental retardation successfully on a truly significant scale [pp. 8–9].

What have been overlooked, misconstrued, or obfuscated by the experts, however, are the implications of these findings for both theories about and the treatment of "mental retardates." Theory reconstruction and treatment programs, therefore, are the foci of the next chapter.

CHAPTER

7

Mental Retardation Revisited

Were we to test Hansel and Gretel today, they would no doubt be diagnosed as mentally retarded. Their lack of formal education, their rejecting parents, and their general impoverishment would ensure poor performance on intelligence tests. Yet Hansel and Gretel were resourceful, clever, manipulative children, capable of controlling the hostile environment into which they were cast. The parallels between this folktale and the case histories of our subjects are distressingly similar. As a metaphor we have found that this simple tale has more explanatory and descriptive potential than the complex abstractions of our retardation experts.

THE HANSEL AND GRETEL METAPHOR

While the metaphor of mental retardation focuses upon assumed inner defects, the Hansel and Gretel metaphor makes no assumptions concerning the inner nature of man, but focuses instead upon observable social events. According to this metaphor, given certain social conditions, anyone could become a Hansel or Gretel—anyone could become an institutionalized mental retardate.

What exactly are the conditions that can transform a child into a retardate?

The most obvious and most potent condition is that the child is unloved and unwanted by the family or its surrogates (foster or stepparents). This factor transcends any disabilities or abilities of the child. The number of instances where families sacrifice in order to keep their severely handicapped offspring at home are legion. Moreover, wanting and loving a child transcend social and personal characteristics of the parents. Poor, uneducated parents may love and want to care for their children as much as wealthy, educated ones. This, however, does not imply that parental attachment is a universal phenomenon. To the contrary, as our case studies have shown, and as our later discussion will elaborate, many parents do not share these sentiments. They simply do not want to maintain their children.

More often than not, the chasm between the parents and the children is paralleled by that between both parents. Divorce, separation, and desertion are important factors in the ultimate transformation of the child into the defective.

The fragmentation of family life often echoes the relationship between the family and society in general. That is, these families tend to be marginal, living on the outskirts of the mainstream. Society's response to these families constitutes the final step in the transformation process. Welfare agencies, social workers, institutions for the retarded, and the supporting cast of social servants finally label and incarcerate the unwanted child. Surely, rejection alone is not sufficient to warrant the title of retardation. Society's contribution is to finalize the transformation by turning the unwanted child into the mentally defective child.

FROM METAPHOR TO MODEL

The most consistent and unambiguous finding after a century of research concerning the institutionalized members of our society (such as mental patients, retardates, and prisoners) is that almost all come from the lower class. This does not mean that poverty alone can account for the putative personal defects or the incarceration of individuals, but it appears to be a necessary condition. Obviously not all of the poor become "labeled" or "imprisoned." This dubious notoriety is conferred upon those members of the lower class who become in some way "negatively visible" to the rest of society. By "negative visibility" we mean that certain people behave in such a way as to violate, threaten, or disrupt the values and propriety norms of the mainstream of society. For instance, a person who breaks laws or acts in a bizarre and frightening fashion becomes visible in a highly negative way. More subtle violations, however, can include a child thrust upon society simply because he is unwanted. This child, through no act or defect of his own, becomes an embarrassment to the community as well as a financial burden. His parents have violated a norm (their socially ascribed roles) so entrenched that it has achieved the status of an unspoken truth, namely, that parents not only cherish their children but are solely responsible for their maintenance. If society recognizes the parents' lack of filial devotion the parents might be imprisoned for their nonsupport or abusive conduct toward the child. But often the sins of the parents are visited upon the child in a more insidious fashion. In our society a cost is exacted from the child whom we *must* maintain. The cost usually takes the form of labeling him "mentally retarded" or "mentally ill." While imprisonment has a set period of time and cost, the label is a burden the child must carry throughout his life. In any case, both the parents and the child have achieved negative visibility.

Most often, however, society neglects to see the parents' actual role in the ultimate incarceration of their child, and, tragically, the child carries the full weight of his being unwanted: he is transformed into a cultural-familial retardate. The labeling of the child, then, exonerates the parents (except perhaps genetically) and society for putting these children away in warehouses for human debris. Thus, a less than average IQ plus parental complaints is all that is needed for the transformation process to begin. The final transformation of the child is an outcome of the interactions between the family and society, and of both with the child.

An attempt to formalize and detail the characteristics of these interactions now will be presented.

THE PARENTS' ROLE IN THE TRANSFORMATION
OF CHILD TO RETARDATE

Even under the best conditions, when children are wanted and valued by the parents, the entry of a new child exacts from the family an economic and psychological price. For the family that is able to afford children (economically and emotionally), the rewards of having a child exceed the costs. Here we can anticipate that the child will experience at the least a benign milieu and that he will be maintained by his parents. If, however, the costs of having and maintaining a child greatly exceed the rewards, the probability that the child will be abused, rejected, and ultimately discarded will be high. This appeared to be the case with our Hansels and Gretels—the rewards as compared to the costs to the parents were low.

The parental reward-cost ratio, a significant factor in the transformation, has several determinants. Obviously, one important set of factors in determining a child's cost to its parents are the personal values and qualities of the parents themselves. If, for example, parents do not adhere to particular cultural values (for example, love thy children), do not want to have children, are overburdened by life's demands, and are rootless and disheveled, the entry of a child into their sphere of influence can only have a disastrous effect on their already precarious existence. From their perspective, the child is an irritant, an unwelcome guest whom they cannot or simply refuse to accept. The dramatic increase in the cost to their lives leads, no doubt, to the maltreatment, rejection, and final ejection of the child. It is not surprising, then, to find in the life histories of our subjects the occurrence of incest, beatings, malnourishment, much less parental concern for their child's education.

The parents' values are in turn determined, to a large extent, by social factors, one of the most important of which is the societal creation and maintenance of "surplus populations" (see Farber, 1968)—populations that contain the majority of the parents of the retarded, populations that are the primary contributors of children to institutions. As we use the term here, surplus populations refer to people who are of no use to the productive capacity of a society. They are persons who are unwilling to participate, incapable of participation, or not wanted in the ongoing activities of cultural life. Farber (1968) describes the composition of the surplus population as complex, drawing members from many segments of society:

> The so-called culturally disadvantaged are included in the surplus population, but the surplus population is by no means restricted to them. Many persons who are surplus from an organizational point of view have become so through old age, genetic factors, chronic illness, or personal misfortune. Harrington includes in "the other America" the human rejects in skid row, the victims of technological unemployment, the property-owning poor in rural areas, Mexican and Anglo migratory workers, unskilled Negro and hillbilly migrants to the city, the aged, and the physically and emotionally disabled. . . . At any rate, a large segment of the American population (perhaps 20 to 25%) may be organizationally surplus or in the process of becoming part of the surplus population [p. 11].

In the next section more attention will be devoted to this concept. For now we will focus upon one outcome of being an adult member of the surplus population: specifically, one's life chances.

Farber (1968) states that "the very idea of an organization-ally surplus population suggests that life chances of the people in this group are minimal. Without participating in the major institutions of the society, the surplus population has no hope of attaining high social status [p. 14]." Thus, the future offers no hope of financial, social, or emotional gain to the "surplus" adult, merely futility and despair. Their reward-cost ratio is fixed before the entry of a child into their lives. The cost of life already exceeds its rewards. This social condition may predispose and facilitate the adults' eventual ejection, or, at the very least, their rejection of the child who intrudes upon their lives.

Before a child is born, then, society guarantees that he will inherit membership into the surplus population. It is without surprise, therefore, that studies of admission rates of the educa-ble and mildly retarded (Farber, 1968) show that the rates were sensitive to economic cycles of prosperity and depression. Specifically, the greatest percentage of admissions occurred during the period of depression, and with the emergence of full employment, it decreased significantly.

Aside from the parents' perception and evaluation of chil-dren in the abstract, the child himself may contribute to the costs of maintenance. For example, if a child is born with some noticeable defect, this can alter considerably the reward-cost ratio. Or if the child gets into trouble in the community or is a nuisance to the parents, cost factors can increase. Very often when children reach puberty, fear of or actual occurrence of pregnancy and other sexual misbehavior can increase the cost of maintenance enough to initiate parental ejection of the child. A large number of our subjects were admitted to the training schools during their adolescence for just those reasons. Physi-cal attributes such as strength for boys and beauty for girls can alter the parental ratios as well. For the boy who will be unable to contribute economically because of a physical disabil-ity, or the girl who will be rejected by potential employers or suitors because she is very unattractive, the cost ratio may be dramatically increased.

In short, the costs of life are so high and the rewards so low for large segments of our population that they are predisposed to reject and, when possible, eject their children. It is not a self-evident truth, then, that all parents love and wish to care for their young.

Our discussion so far has focused on the poor, surplus parent —and with good reason, since they contribute the most children to the institutions we studied. Their middle-class counterparts, nonetheless, deserve some attention. We do not believe that the more affluent members of our society love or cherish their children more than the lower class. Child maintenance, however, is an easier task and is less of a burden for the more affluent. Planned parenthood, economic security, and social status in the community all help raise the reward-to-cost ratio for new middle-class parents, making it easier to maintain children or to absorb costs that may occur over time.

More important, however, are the alternatives available to the middle-class parents who want to eject their children. These alternative paths of ejection are subtle and disguised; so disguised, in fact, that the ejection may be seen as a "virtue." For instance, the middle-class child who is a disciplinary problem, who is not doing well in school, or who is not loved can be sent to a military academy or a boarding school. The emotional costs of maintaining the child can be reduced considerably by utilizing these socially sanctioned and valued institutions. The poor, however, do not have the same avenues available for ridding themselves of their children—for them there is only the wilderness of the vast state institutions.

It is evident that parent-child relationships can be understood only in the context of social, economic, political, and ideological forces. We have just examined how these social forces act on the parents and affect their responses to their children. Now we will examine how society responds to that which it has created: surplus adults and children.

SOCIAL FACTORS IN THE TRANSFORMATION

Although it appears at first that large groups of marginal, surplus people overburden society, closer examination reveals just how valuable they may be. Surely a society can function with-

out the existence of such groups, but, as Farber (1968) point
out, the presence of surplus populations "contributes to main
taining the existing social structure in at least three ways: first
they generate a series of special institutions; second, they make
possible the effective operation of the basic social institutions o:
the society; and third, they aid in the perpetuation of the socia
classes [p. 13]."

The first contribution implies what many already know: tha
armies of well-paid middle-class people are required to super
vise and service the lower class. Social scientists, medical doc
tors, psychiatrists, lawyers, social workers, and so on all may
benefit from the existence of surplus, marginal people. In short
very large numbers of professional people, as well as nonpro-
fessionals, owe their economic and social status to the surplus
population. The importance of this group to the economic
security of the middle class has been noted by Farber (1968):
"The number of persons presently engaged in handling problems related to surplus populations in the United States is large
enough so that there would be serious economic dislocations if
all organizationally superfluous individuals were to be removed
from society [p. 13]."

Surplus populations serve society in another way. They allow
the established middle and upper classes the prerogative of
choice and power, particularly in the selection of job applicants.
The term surplus population indicates that we have more applicants for lower-level jobs than we need. The resultant wide
latitude of choice increases the social power of the chooser, enabling him to establish criteria irrelevant to the job in question
(for example, a high-school diploma for a street cleaner). He
may by so doing exercise his power and elevate his self-esteem
at the expense of the lower class.

A related contribution of the surplus population is that they
help to maintain a stable social order. The presence of a per-
sistent, nonmobile lower class buffers the changes in the rest
of the social order. Moreover, having such a population serves
as a negative example for the middle-class person who may
lack the motivation to "make good." Other contributions of the
surplus population can be cited, but we think our point has
been made: namely, that surplus people are not necessarily a

cost to society. To the contrary, they appear at least in our society to help rather than hinder the smooth functioning of the
social machinery.

We believe that their contributions to society may in part
explain why, despite our vast wealth and resourcefulness, surplus populations have been allowed and, in many instances, encouraged to exist. The inertia toward ridding society of marginal people can be seen, then, as a function of society's reward-
cost ratio. Simply, the cost to society for the maintenance of
the surplus does not exceed its rewards.

If we view surplus populations, then, as a valued commodity,
it becomes clear why the behavior of this group is so often
misconstrued (for example, the belief that poor performance on
an IQ test by a marginal child indicates mental retardation).
Such misconstructions serve society by stigmatizing and thus
perpetuating the existence of this population. This is most
clearly illustrated by our cultural definition of deviancy. If a
person is not a smoothly functioning member of the mainstream, a cog in the vast wheel of society, he is a deviant. Thus
any member of the surplus population is by definition a deviant, since he is not a member of the mainstream. On a more
molecular level, behavior that is valued by society at large is
seen as "intelligent," "rational," "meaningful," "mature," and
"constructive." On the other hand, behaviors valued by the
subculture of the lower class are "stupid," "irrational," "mean-
ingless," "immature," and "destructive." To be born into the
surplus population, then, is to be born a deviant.

Enmeshed in this tautological definition of deviancy are the
criteria society has established for entrance into the mainstream, most of which guarantee that members of the surplus
will remain surplus. A good example of a criterion that allows
society not only to identify but also to exclude members of the
disreputable poor from entering the mainstream is IQ. The
cultural bias of IQ tests is by now a well-worn finding. We
know that surplus people will do poorly on standard intelligence tests, yet we administer these tests, find low IQ scores
among this group and, thus, exclude them from participation
in the important institutions of our society.

Dexter (1962), disconcerted over this state of affairs, remarked that "there is also the experience which may be observed over and over again of the denial of employment, of legal rights, of a fair hearing, of an opportunity, to the stupid (i.e., have a low IQ or show poor academic performance), and not because the stupidity is relevant to the task, or claim, or situation." It indeed seems bizarre that an enlightened society should place emphasis upon an IQ test when it makes contact with a child who has experienced in his few years of life humiliation, beatings, starvation, sexual assault, and other degradations. To use this test score to define the basic nature of the child and to determine the fate of his life, shows, in the very least, an irresponsible attitude toward the child. The job of society, then, is to keep its house in order by identifying its deviants and excluding them forever from the mainstream.

Misconstructions appear at still another level. It is one thing to identify and control the deviant, and another to state the cause of his deviancy. Deviancy, in our society, is seen primarily as a function of some inner defect. Earlier in this century, the inner defect was attributed to the lower-than-human position on the phylogenetic scale occupied by the disreputable poor. That is, in Social Darwinian terms, the poor were seen as somewhat less than human. More recently, the cause of the inner defect has been viewed in terms of the "social germ" theory (see Chapter 1). According to this interpretation, the poor are defective organisms not because of their genetic structure but because of what life has done to them. What is common to both interpretations is that they share the belief that there exist inner defects which exclude people from meaningful and successful participation in society.

It is striking indeed that despite the multitude of theories concerning the problems of the surplus population, no major position has ever been taken which suggests that the poor are not failures, defectives, or deviants but rather are pretty much like the rest of us. That is, given similar circumstances, anyone would behave as the disreputable poor behave. The commitment to the defect notion is ingrained strongly not only in society's response to the lower class but in our professional theories and practices as well.

The social scientists and professionals involved in problem areas (for example, mental illness and mental retardation) concerning mostly persons from the surplus poor have served to perpetuate, while making more sophisticated, the prejudices of the mainstream. As a result, they have not only assisted society in its housekeeping chores, they have enlarged considerably the domain of their own influence as well. For example, it has never been fashionable to be poor, but at one time in our history the poor were seen simply as being poor. Half-hearted attempts to help them sustain life were made, usually taking the form of almshouses and similar refuges. What is most striking is that these nineteenth-century institutions housed individuals whose social circumstances were decidedly similar to those of our present-day mental retardates and mental patients.

The misconstruction can be illustrated further by tracing the history of the transformation of an almshouse into a mental institution. Stearns and Ullman (1949) in their review of the history of the state mental institution at Tewksbury, Massachusetts, remind us that it originally served as a refuge for the lame, the infirm, and the poor. The administration at that time was entirely in the hands of nonmedical personnel. The transformation of this refuge into a medical facility is important not so much because it illustrates how institutions may change, but rather how people may be transformed from the poor to the "mentally ill."

Concerning the institutional transformation, Stearns and Ullman write:

> . . . the last 94 years has seen the constant withdrawal from the unsettled poor classification into the medical classification. In 1869, despite the institution of public care for the insane, there was still a large component of such cases, and buildings were erected for these. . . . By 1883 the superintendent was a physician and since then the medical features have grown, until in 1900 the name was changed from State Almshouse to State Hospital; in 1909, from State Hospital to State Infirmary; and finally, in 1939, to Tewksbury State Hospital and Infirmary. Gradually caretakers were replaced by nurses and the supervision became medical [pp. 803–809].

What about the people? Have they, over the years, change substantially with respect to psychiatric criteria? A surve conducted in 1843 showed, according to nineteenth-centur standards, that only 30 percent of the persons residing in suc public institutions were "insane." At the outset these institution housed primarily the "unsettled poor," immigrants, children and the jobless. Tewksbury along with two other almshouse were constructed specifically in response to the influx of Iris immigrants to Massachusetts following the famine of 184€ Stearns and Ullman, on the basis of interviews of the new ad missions to Tewksbury, describe the present-day residents a follows:

> The individuals show an excess of immigrants, a deficit in forma education, in occupational skill, and in marital success. We do no find a preponderance of catastrophic illness, but we do fin alcohol to have been an important factor in the failure of thes individuals to make a successful adaptation. . . . It is not pos sible to squeeze them into categories of mental disease howeve much elasticity we may be willing to use. Yet they have neve functioned successfully in a competitive society. Their relative and friends would have nothing to do with them; they have wor them out or shamed them to the point where they wished n further contact [p. 808].

The similarity of residents, despite the institutional changes leads one to conclude that the "mentally ill" of today are the social descendants of the nineteenth-century poor. What once was perceived as impoverished and futile life circumstances ha been transformed into a more potent stigma, mental defects.

The transformation of lower-class persons' behavior into in dexes of mental disruption or defect is, as Miller, Riessman and Seagull (1968) point out, a distressingly prevalent phe nomenon. The typical stereotype of the poor is that they are in capable of managing their own affairs, are like children because they cannot control their impulses, are irresponsible, and lac character. In the more sophisticated realm of the social science this stereotype is echoed in the concept of "deferred gratifica tion pattern" (DGP). Deferred gratification pattern, write

Miller and others, "has been in the first rank of principles explaining 'lower class behavior.' Indeed, it is probably the most frequently used element in the discussion of lower class life. Its presumed absence in the non-middle classes is regarded as a barrier to improvement among this population, and, for some, an explanation of why the poor are poor [p. 416]."

According to Miller and others, most experts on the poor believe that the middle class is able to defer impulse gratification through the strategy of "impulse renunciation," while the poor, having no such device available, are "impulse followers." Because they cannot defer gratification, the catalogue of the lower classes' "impulse following" behaviors is rather extensive:

> . . . relative readiness to engage in physical violence, free sexual expression (as through intercourse), minimum pursuit of education, low aspiration level, failure of parents to identify the class of their children's playmates, free spending, little emphasis on being well-mannered and obedient, and short time dependence of parents. On the other hand, middle class persons feel that they *should* save, postpone, and renounce a variety of gratifications. . . . It is important to realize that an undertone of the DGP analysis is that the pattern is not temporary nor easily overcome. Indeed the assumption is that the ability or inability to defer gratification is deeply embedded in the personality dynamics of the individual, performing an important role in the psychodynamic economy. The picture seems to be that the DGP or the non-DGP are developed through early life experiences, they become incorporated in the personality and are relatively impervious to situational factors [pp. 416–419].

Miller and others' (1968) careful scrutiny of the literature lead them to disagree with the above assumptions about and interpretations of the behavior of the lower-class people. Aside from finding that researches conducted on the deferred gratification pattern "do not instill confidence in the sweeping conclusions of the DGP," they were concerned that the "DGP emphasis leads to social policies which emphasize 'rehabilitation' rather than expanding opportunity." This is a point to which we will return shortly.

In short, society's response to the surplus poor is to stigmatize them (with a helpful hand from the professionals) by invoking putative inner defects in order to explain why their behavior is different from that of the mainstream. The first step in this process is to misconstrue the meaning of lower-class behavior and to create a negative myth about the basic "nature" of the poor. After they have been defined as deviant, criteria which offer evidence of their deficiencies are constructed, which, in turn, allow for their exclusion from meaningful participation in society.

This procedure is, in fact, identical to the steps taken to transform a child into a mental retardate.

THE CHILD AND THE TRANSFORMATION

By now it should be clear that the child need do nothing but be born of parents from the surplus population to be suspect intellectually, emotionally, and motivationally. The description of the poor have been echoed in the literature concerning mental retardation. Mental retardates, among other things, are believed to be: incapable of managing their own affairs, unable to control their impulses, irresponsible and lacking in character, ready to engage in physical violence, and little interested in the pursuit of education. The child of the surplus poor, then, is a potential retardate lacking only the formal recognition of his "defectiveness."

The "recognition" occurs as soon as the child is separated from his family either by their choice or on the basis of decisions made by social agents. The reason the child's "defectiveness" *must* be seen now is explicated below.

The poor, discarded, or extracted child may be placed in one of several refuges: foster homes, children's shelters, orphanages, mental institutions, or training schools for the retarded. Since all but the last facility can absorb a very limited number of children, the vast majority are sent to the largest catchment area, the training schools for the retarded. It is no surprise then that they become "recognized" (diagnosed) as mental re-

:dates. How else can society justify the children's inclusion
:o a milieu for defectives?

For the bulk of these youngsters, the label of mental retarda-
›n comes after the fact—after society decides that these chil-
en *must* be put in training schools. The basis for admission,
en, is not the children's intellectual capacity or social adjust-
ent, but merely their dependency on the state for their well-
·ing and maintenance.

The steps in the sequence of social sanitation and stigmatiza-
›n often lead to one outcome we have yet to examine: the
iild labeled mentally retarded may, as a result, begin to *act*
:arded. The reasons for this seeming "self-fulfilling prophecy"
⁄Ierton, 1967) may be varied: one child may wish to please
s "labelers" or, rather, not displease them by acting intel-
ȝent; another, in order not to "rock the boat" by disturbing
1d threatening his keepers (attendants and matrons) with
:telligent behavior, may be forced to act stupid; still another
ay want to act retarded in order to ensure that he will not
₂ sent home, that he may be able to stay in the reasonably
able, secure environment of the training school. These reasons
ıve been given credibility by the "retardates" in their inter-
ews (see Appendix A).

The social performance of individuals, as we well know,
determined to a large extent by the expectations of the audi-
ıce. The "retardates," then, are obeying a rather simple law
 human behavior. The best summary of the process may be
·und in Tannenbaum's (1938) description of the "dramatiza-
›n of evil"; the reader need only substitute such a term as
ıental retardate or schizophrenic for the term criminal in Tan-
ɛnbaum's following selection:

> The first dramatization of "evil" which separates the child out
> of his group for specialized treatment plays a greater role in
> making the criminal [retardate] than perhaps any other expe-
> rience. It cannot be too often emphasized that for the child the
> whole situation has become different. He now lives in a different
> world. He has been tagged. A new and hitherto nonexistent en-
> vironment has been precipitated out for him.

The process of making the criminal [retardate], therefore, i process of tagging, defining, identifying, segregating, describi emphasizing, making conscious and self-conscious; it become way of stimulating, suggesting, emphasizing, and evolving very traits that are complained of [pp. 19–20].

The roles played by educators, psychologists, psychiatri: pediatricians, social workers, and other "helping" profession in the metamorphosis of the child is obvious. Just as they t wittingly transform the adult debris into emotional defecti (for example, schizophrenics), they transform the discard young into mental defectives (for example, cultural-famil retardates).

The process of social sanitation that we have describ above, including the interaction between the family and ciety, and both with the child is represented in Figure 2.

SOME THEORETICAL IMPLICATIONS

The portrait of the retardate that has emerged in this book that of an adept, rational, sensitive, resourceful, and int ligent human being. In Chapter 3 we found that they not o acquired a manipulative interpersonal orientation, but t they were able to carry out successfully subtle manipulati strategies. They were capable of protecting their self-intere by using complex tactics of impression management, such ingratiating themselves with the staff, and controlling their test scores in order to appear either "bright" or "dull."

Chapter 4 demonstrated that within the confines of t training schools, these youngsters were able to control a exploit their somewhat hostile environment in order to li the way they personally desired. Many of the retardates we able even to implement life styles that were counter to t values of the institutions. Moreover, the styles of adaptati were associated with characteristics of the retardates such age, sex, and their attitudes about retardation, and are r at all related to differential institutional demands or "level intellectual functioning" (as assessed by the institution).

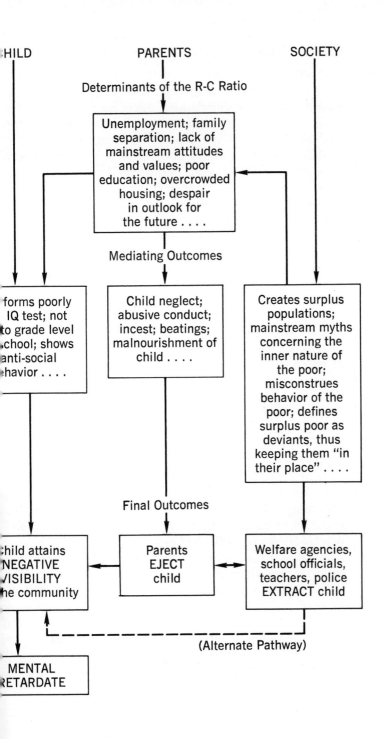

CHILD | PARENTS | SOCIETY

Determinants of the R-C Ratio

Unemployment; family separation; lack of mainstream attitudes and values; poor education; overcrowded housing; despair in outlook for the future . . . .

Mediating Outcomes

forms poorly IQ test; not to grade level school; shows anti-social behavior . . . .

Child neglect; abusive conduct; incest; beatings; malnourishment of child . . . .

Creates surplus populations; mainstream myths concerning the inner nature of the poor; misconstrues behavior of the poor; defines surplus poor as deviants, thus keeping them "in their place" . . . .

Final Outcomes

Child attains NEGATIVE VISIBILITY he community

Parents EJECT child

Welfare agencies, school officials, teachers, police EXTRACT child

(Alternate Pathway)

MENTAL RETARDATE

Conflicts between the modal attitudes of the retardates and those of the staff were described in Chapter 5. The attitudes of the retardates, particularly their desire for the training school to be nondemanding and pleasant so that they could have freedom to enjoy their stay, and their belief that they were not particularly stupid or defective, or even different from most people, were diametrically opposed to the beliefs of the staff. The results of that chapter made it clear that the styles of adaptation the retardates evolved were, indeed, hard-won victories. Although most of the retardates spent more than half their lives in an institution which fostered images of their defectiveness and helplessness, they were able to resist effectively the negative, degrading image. They maintained, instead, both in action and attitude, their competence and humanness.

The reasons for incarceration and the family histories of the retardates were examined in Chapter 6. Both sources, the retardates and the social case workers, depicted clearly why children are sent to institutions for the mentally retarded—because of rejection, family disintegration, or betrayal rather than because of stupidity or defectiveness. Indeed, we found little that was stupid or defective about these youngsters.

These empirical findings and our model lead to one conclusion: the concept of mental retardation must be discarded entirely. It has no scientific value whatever, merely serving to obfuscate and distort the meaning of the behavior of the rejected child. It has no humanitarian value, but instead stigmatizes and victimizes youngsters for social events over which they have little or no control. Moreover, this concept has led to enormous expenditures of time, effort, and money in a useless search for psychic factors when the real problems exist in society.

It is obvious, at this point, that we have left the traditional realm of psychology and have entered the sociopolitical arena. We have done this because "mental retardation" is, in fact, sociopolitical, not a psychological, construct. The myth perpetrated by a society which refuses to recognize the true nature of its needed social reforms, has successfully camouflaged the politics of diagnosis and incarceration. This has been discussed fully in the preceding pages and need not be reiterated

The point we want to make is that the attention of social scientists should not turn toward a search for a new metaphor to replace mental retardation. Indeed, to continue to foist upon the public myths concerning putative inner defects is to neglect one's responsibility as a scientist as well as a humanist concerned with the needs of man.

Some may argue that mental retardates as well as the poor in general are in fact different from the rest of us; thus to neglect to study these differences and the etiology of them would be irresponsible. But surely no one would disagree that the poor are different from the affluent just as professors are different from bank presidents, Republicans different from Democrats, Americans different from Swedes. The significant factor is not that differences exist between groups of people, but how society evaluates the differences. The evaluation is clearly a political and moral enterprise, unworthy of the scientific respectability it has been given.

Social scientists in fields other than psychology have demonstrated just how useful it is theoretically to broaden one's perspective and include the political when engaged in the study of human behavior (Goffman, 1959; 1961; Etzioni, 1968; Merton, 1967; Scheff, 1966, to name a few). Although there seems to be a growing concern with the social context of behavior among psychologists and psychiatrists, close inspection reveals that they still dwell primarily in the molecular realm of the intrapsychic. Thus, despite "new" theories, empirical studies, and treatment programs in this field, lip service only is paid to the societal aspects of the problem—the spotlight remains on the deviant in question and, particularly, the status of his mind.

By moving from the traditional, although admittedly secure, realm of psychiatry and psychology to an objective analysis of the politics of deviancy, new and exciting contributions may be made. Creative theoretical and research innovations would provide more than what we have now: pseudo-answers to misconstrued questions. Moreover, the management and "treatment" of deviants would take on new forms, forms that would no longer dehumanize and degrade the recipients of our professional "help."

TREATMENT IMPLICATIONS OF OUR MODEL

The results of our research program, in addition to studi
conducted by others, not only contradict the widely held a
sumptions about mental retardation, but support strongly o
theoretical position as well. We believe there is nothing pa
ticularly different about "retardates," but that they are ve
much like everyone else. They do not, therefore, belong in a
specialized institutions such as training schools. If we spe
now, as we must, of rejected rather than retarded children, tl
treatment implications are not immediately obvious. Thus,
order to dispel any distortions or misinterpretations of our po
tion, the implications of our work will be presented in detail.

First, our indictment of the current theories of retardatic
as well as the practices of their exponents in no way impli
that there should not be institutions for these children. Sure
after seeing the backgrounds from which the bulk of the
youngsters come, it would be criminal to insist that they stay
a home where they are humiliated, abused, and degrade
Parents who do not wish to or who cannot maintain their chi
dren should be provided with opportunities for the disposal
their responsibilities. Moreover, children should be remove
from homes where they are severely abused physically and ps
chologically. The channels society now provides, however, off
no respite for the child, who is thrust into institutions where l
is treated, albeit more subtly, in much the same manne
Viewed by the staff as homogeneous, defective, maladaptive o
ganisms, these youngsters find themselves once again in
milieu where they are humiliated, degraded, and, at time
abused.

In addition, we do not mean to imply that the institutions fo
the "retarded" are homogeneous. In our travels we observe
an array of institutions ranging from overtly hostile, restrictiv
and authoritarian settings to beatific surroundings. In a
places, however, the residents were seen as retardates—a pe
ception which cannot help but exert a negative influence on th
youngsters.

Although we have focused throughout the book on the fami
ial-cultural (educable, nonorganic) retardate, much of wh

we have said as well as what we will be saying, we feel, is applicable to the brain-damaged child, who also has been bestowed with the label "mental retardate." The cost to the parents of maintaining an organically impaired child is, no doubt, greater than the others we described. These children very often are rejected because the parents cannot (rather than do not want to) maintain or care for their children. But here again, there is no place for such children except the institutions for the retarded—thus, they are labeled, incarcerated, and treated for their retardation. There is no reason, however, to assume that mental retardation is a relevant concept even for brain-damaged children. That is, we believe that here too the concept serves only to distort and obfuscate the meaning of the actual disability. That these children are different is unquestionable; that they are deficient mentally, however, remains to be seen. There have been cases cited which have shown that in an enriched, rewarding milieu even severely brain-damaged or genetically impaired (Mongoloid) children can function normally in many respects. Moreover, it is ludicrous to use the label "mental retardate" for the profoundly brain-damaged child who cannot function at all on any psychological or physical level. For example, one would hardly label a man in a comatose state "mentally retarded" because he cannot function intelligently. The label again obfuscates reality. Our proposed solution to the treatment of the retarded (which falls short of dramatic and needed social reforms) includes, therefore, not only the cultural-familial retardate but the genetically or organically damaged child as well.

COOPERATIVE RETREATS: OUR PROPOSED SOLUTION

In our earlier work with mental patients (Braginsky and others, 1969) we proposed that mental hospitals be abandoned and, in their place, cooperative retreats be established. These retreats were seen as offering temporary relief from the stresses of life ("to get away from it all") for some, while providing a permanent refuge for others who cannot or do not want to "make it" in our complex, demanding society (for example, members

of the surplus population, the lame, the aged). Support for th
cooperative retreats would come initially from the public an
private sources that now fund mental hospitals, homes for th
aged, training schools for the retarded, and other places of s
cial sanitation.

Because the retreat is not a "treatment" facility, thereb
nullifying the *raison d'etre* of psychologists, psychiatrists an
other "helping" professionals, they would be coordinated,
the outset, by hotel management personnel. The staff wou
include also teachers, artisans, musicians, and others who cou
provide services that would enhance the experience of the res
dents. Persons who would choose to use the retreat as a pe
manent home could, in time, take over the running of the r
treat so that, ultimately, it could become a self-governing cor
munity. In addition, products made in workshops or from farn
ing could become a source of income for the community,
well as providing meaningful, enjoyable work for the residen

In short, situated in the countryside, these retreats wou
have facilities for the enrichment and enhancement of tho
who come for a short time as well as those who remain for lor
periods. The cooperative retreat, therefore, would be an expe
ment in living where persons would have the opportunity, ev
for a short while, to be members of a small, stable, and dem
cratic community. Such a setting would encourage the explor
tion of one's potential, leading to a more personally satisfyir
existence.

With respect to the rejected children, additional faciliti
would be required. Foster parents, recruited from the perm
nent residents, would live in cottages with a small number
the children. The education of the children, aside from the bas
skills, would be formalized as little as possible, emphasizir
personal enrichment rather than conformity of knowledge. Mo
important, perhaps, is that no labels would be attached to th
children, no burden of defectiveness to overcome in order
realize their life goals. Swimming pools, libraries, music rec
tals, movies, and so on would be utilized by both the childr
and the adults.

Retreats such as these would free society from misdirectir
its energies and resources in support of myths. The eliminatic

of the "myth of mental illness," the "myth of mental deficiency," and the entire mythology concerning the surplus poor will remove the camouflage which has obscured for too long the crucial problems facing society. Researchers as well as practitioners will be able to direct their attention toward more meaningful endeavors. And, perhaps more important, regardless of personal attributes and endowments, society could no longer view people as just so much refuse which it must rid itself of. The machinery of social sanitation, the concept of "less than human," would no longer be perpetrated by a complacent society. Instead, the unwanted and unneeded members of the human community would be given the opportunity to do more than merely survive.

APPENDIX A

Interviews*

NAME: *Lynn Brown* AGE: *21* SEX: *Female*
LENGTH OF TIME IN TRAINING SCHOOL: *5 years*
DIAGNOSIS: *Mild retardation*

Q. How do you typically spend your day here in the school?

A. Five o'clock I get up. I get to breakfast around 6. Then I go to the workshop until 11:30. Then I have lunch. After that I go to the hospital at one and work there until 6. Then I go back to the building and talk to the girls until about 9 o'clock when you have to go to bed.

Q. Do you have any days off?

A. Saturday. I get up at 5:30 to go to breakfast, and then I do private things, like wash my clothes and iron. I listen to records. After lunch I go downstairs and watch TV. I stay in the building all day, even when the weather is nice. We can't go to other buildings. We can sit outside, but we really can't go places. We really don't have a lot of freedom.

Q. Are there any advantages in being here?

A. No.

---

* The interviews have been edited, but the language of the subjects has not been altered.

Q. What's this place for?

A. The mentally retarded.

Q. Do you consider yourself retarded?

A. No. Otherwise I wouldn't be able to work.

Q. Do you think the other girls in the building are retarded?

A. Not all of them. Most of them are not retarded.

Q. Why are you here?

A. I'm not saying. It's my personal business.

Q. If you could, would you leave tomorrow?

A. I sure would.

Q. Have you seen people here who are called retarded but they are really bright?

A. We are all called retarded, so I guess so.

Q. Are any of the girls here as smart as some of the attendants?

A. Some of them are smarter. The attendants don't like it. They don't like me because I tell them off. They want us to behave and not tell them off or swear. Some of us girls can go out and get a better job than they have and they know it. Some of the girls can typewrite and can get a job as secretary. They have the training for that. Even I can hold a job.

Q. Are there some people here who want to stay?

A. They're crazy if they do. Some do, but not me. I want to get out of here. The girls I hang around with want to get out. Some of us bright girls know we can hold a job and want to get out of here because the attendants put too much on us. They know we are good workers.

Q. Why would some girls not want to leave?

A. Because they don't know what a home is, I guess, and they think this place is the only one.

NAME: *Emily Taylor* AGE: *23* SEX: FEMALE
LENGTH OF TIME IN TRAINING SCHOOL: *6 years*
DIAGNOSIS: *Borderline*

Q. How do you typically spend your time here at the training school?

A. I try to get up at 6 o'clock, but I usually get up a few minutes later. I get to breakfast about 6:30. I work in the kitchen at Brian Hall. I work there from 7 until 3. Then I come back to the building and wait until suppertime. I watch television in the dayroom with a bunch of girls. I'll talk once in a while. After supper I get ready for bed, about 6 o'clock. I don't usually go to bed until 8:30. Between 6 and 8:30 I have a smoke and talk with the girls. I like to talk with them. We talk about the day and boys and things like that. All girls talk about boys. On weekends I like to go to work because there's nothing to do around here—just hang around and work around the house. Most of the work is usually done in the morning so you have to hang around all day. I wish I could work on Saturday and Sunday. Saturday morning I clean the store room. I start before breakfast and finish about 9. Then I hang around. I go outside and sit down by myself. I like to be by myself—it keeps me out of arguments. At 11 I come in and get ready for dinner. There's a good story on television on Saturday afternoons, so I go and watch after dinner. About 4 I get ready for supper. After supper I get ready for bed. I do anything I can find to do between 6 and 9:30 —watch television, find a book to read and talk. Mostly be by myself.

Q. Why do you think you are here?

A. That's a good question. I don't know. Well, I thought at first I was put here for schooling to learn how to work. But gee whiz, I have been out of school for three years now. I'm working and I should know how to work by now.

Q. Then why do you think you are here?

A. I don't like to talk about it. It's something I did. It was a mistake, but everyone makes mistakes. That's why I think I am here. My mother and my father never told me, but I kind of guessed it. It happened when I was sixteen—it happened.

Q. What would you be doing if there was no place like this?

A. Probably hanging around the house, cleaning it for my step-mother.

Q. Are there any advantages in being in a place like this?

A. Well, there are some things here I like in this place that I don't like about the outside. Well, it doesn't have to do with the whole outside—it's partly a family thing. I like to feel that these people here are my family. I don't have this on the outside.

Q. What is this place for?

A. At first I thought it was for just the sick. But everybody else that has been coming in here are fine. I don't know what it's for. There are a lot of sick here, but there are a lot that could be out too.

Q. If you could, would you leave this place tomorrow without hesitation?

A. I've asked myself that lots of times and I really don't know. Sometimes I want to and sometimes I feel that I want to stay here.

Q. Are there people who are considered retarded here, but who are really bright, who act so as to make others think that they are stupid?

A. Yes. I think they want to act stupid so that they don't have to worry about some of the things on the outside, the way they live on the outside, the way they have to do this and that. They just feel they can get everything free here. They don't want to take the responsibilities outside. They can also get waited on hand and foot. I hate a person like that.

Q. Are there any kids here who are as bright as the attendants?

A. Some of them.

Q. Are there any brighter than the attendants?

A. Yes.

Q. Do you think it would be wise to show an attendant that you are brighter or as bright as he (she)?

A. No. Not really. I don't know what really would happen, but I don't think they should show it. I wouldn't show it unless it was definitely important.

Q. How are you expected to behave by the people who work here?

A. Sometimes I think the attendants expect the retardates to act stupid, because they treat them stupid. They treat them like they were stupid. I don't think some of the attendants here know how to treat a retardate. They don't treat them like they could learn. They push them around and everything else. I've seen it done.

Q. Would you consider most people in this building retarded?

A. Not retarded. Just a very few.

NAME: *Karen Fox*   AGE: *28*   SEX: *Female*
LENGTH OF TIME IN TRAINING SCHOOL: *19 years*
DIAGNOSIS: *Mild retardation*

Q. How do you typically spend your time here at the training school?

A. I get up before 7 o'clock. Then I go to work with the blind children. I work there until 3. I mostly help the blind patients—feed them—change them. After 3 I come back to the building and take care of some errands. After 3:30 I relax. I read on the ward until suppertime around 5. After supper, once in a while I come down and talk with the girls in the dayroom. Well, until I feel like I want to go upstairs, then I go back upstairs, get undressed and washed and lie down. I don't go to sleep until 10. I usually talk with the girls until then. On Saturdays I work with the blind children. I work all morning on Sunday morning. When I finish with the blind children I go to church about 3. Then I come back for the rest of the day.

Q. Why are you here?

A. I don't really know. I believe that I was slow, but I am not sure.

Q. What would you be doing if there wasn't a place like this?

A. Roaming the streets.

Q. Are there any advantages in being in a place like this rather than being outside?

A. Yes. You have a building you can stay in in case any hoodlum is against you. You can't get hurt here. It's a place to live in.

Q. Is there anything you don't like about this place?

A. Not really.

Q. What is this place for?

A. To help the boys and girls. To help them get acquainted with one another.

Q. If you could, would you leave this place tomorrow?

A. Well, if I had the opportunity to get a job, I would leave. But not under any other circumstances.

Q. Are there any kids here who are bright but they act so that people think they are stupid?

A. Yes, there is.

Q. Why would they do this?

A. Well, a lot of them act stupid to get a little attention and sympathy from others. To get someone to pay a little more attention to them instead of the other ones.

Q. Are there any kids here who are as bright as some of the attendants?

A. There are.

Q. Are there any who are brighter than some of the attendants?

A. Yes.

Q. Is it wise to show the attendants that you are as bright as they are?

A. No. It may cause trouble.

Q. How do they expect you to act?

A. To act your age and not to ask for sympathy or attention.

APPENDIX B

Test Forms

IT TEST (TRAINING SCHOOL F)

1. What is the name of a medical doctor at F?
1a. In what building is his or her office located?
2. What is the name of a nurse?
2a. Where is her office located?
3. What is the name of a matron?
3a. What floor is his or her office located on?
4. What is the name of an attendant in your building?
5. What is the name of a psychologist?
5a. Where is his or her office located?
6. What is the name of a social worker?
7. What is the name of the Superintendent of F?
8. How many floors are there in your building?
9. What is the closest building to the administration building?
10. Is the hospital closer to the bakery than the administration building?
11. What is the name of the building in which old women are placed?
12. What is the name of the building in which blind people are kept?
13. What is the name of the building where the nursery is?

14. What is the newest building where retardates live?
15. What is the name of the building where they put boys who get into trouble?
16. What is the name of the building where crippled men are kept?
17. How many canteens are there at F?
17a. What are the names of the buildings where they are located?
18. What is the name of the building where crippled women are kept?
19. Where do they hold dances?
20. Make a guess as to how many people live in your building.
21. In what building are the movies shown?
22. Make a guess as to how many retardates are at F.
23. What time does the evening shift start?
24. What are the names of the buildings where employees live?
25. Who is the head of the social workers?
26. Who is the head of the nurses?
27. Who is the head of the psychology department?
28. Where is the main switchboard?
29. How much vacation time does an attendant get?
30. Where is the occupational therapy department located?

IT TEST (TRAINING SCHOOL M)

1. What is the name of a medical doctor at Mansfield?
1a. In what building is his or her office located?
2. What is the name of a nurse?
2a. Where is her office located?
3. What is the name of a matron?
3a. What floor is her office located on?
4. What is the name of an attendant in your building?
5. What is the name of a psychologist?
5a. Where is his or her office located?
6. What is the name of a social worker?

7. What is the name of the Superintendent of M?
8. How many floors are there in your building?
9. What is the closest building to the administration building?
10. Is D House closer to Athletic Field #1 than K House?
11. What is the name of the hospital?
12. What is the name of the building closest to the laundry?
13. What is the name of the school?
14. Is W Cottage or M Cottage closer to the laundry?
15. What building is closest to the swimming pool?
16. How many athletic fields are there at M?
17. How many canteens are there at M?
17a. What are the names of the buildings where they are located?
18. What is the name of a building near the Power House?
19. Where do they hold dances?
20. Make a guess as to how many people live in your building.
21. In what building are the movies shown?
22. Make a guess as to how many retardates are at M.
23. What time does the evening shift start?
24. What are the names of the buildings where employees live?
25. Who is the head of the social workers?
26. Who is the head of the nurses?
27. Who is the head of the psychology department?
28. Where is the main switchboard?
29. How much vacation time does an attendant get?
30. Where is the occupational therapy department located?

PRIVATE SCHOOL FOR RETARDED
OPINIONS ABOUT THE SCHOOL

1. The staff at the school never makes mistakes about anything.
2. Every single house-parent in the cottages is as good to us as a mother and father would be to their child.

3. The food I have had in the cottage is as good, if not better, than food in a good restaurant.
4. Since I have been here, I have never been asked to do things I didn't like.
5. There is nothing about the school that needs improvement of any kind.
6. The treatment here sometimes makes a student ill.
7. Some of the rules of the school are really not necessary.
8. Sometimes I have thought that the school doesn't help some of the students.
9. There were times that I did things in the school that the teachers and house-parents didn't know about.
10. I sometimes cover up my true feelings when I talk to the teachers and house-parents.
11. I like everyone I ever met at the school.
12. I am proud of being a student at this school.
13. Living in this school is almost as nice as living in a good hotel.
14. There is nothing that the school won't do to make a student happy and comfortable.
15. All students who are not allowed to leave the cottage deserve it since the staff is always fair in its decisions.
16. I agree with everything the school wants me to do.
17. There are times when I wish the school treated me better.
18. Sometimes the staff doesn't want to be bothered by the students.
19. There are times when I feel that some of the teachers and house-parents don't quite understand me.
20. Sometimes the school treats the older students as if they were children.
21. This school is not fit for people who need help.
22. I have never had a single decent meal in the cottage.
23. Sometimes the school does some good for the students.
24. There are times when a student needs to be on restriction.
25. There are times when the staff is right even though a student may think it is wrong.
26. There is not a single good thing about being a student in this school.
27. I can't find one interesting thing to do in this school.

28. The school always takes advantage of the students.
29. At times I feel comfortable and happy being in this school.
30. In some ways I get more attention in the school than I got outside.

PUBLIC HIGH SCHOOL
OPINIONS ABOUT THE SCHOOL

1. The teachers I have this term are people who never make mistakes about anything.
2. All my teachers this term are as good and fair to me as my mother or father.
3. The teachers I have this term are as good, if not better, than teachers in a good university.
4. My teachers have never asked me to do things I didn't like.
5. There is nothing about my teachers this term that needs improvement of any kind.
6. My teachers are sometimes unfair to some students.
7. Some of the rules my teachers enforce are really not necessary.
8. Sometimes I have thought that my teachers don't help some of the students.
9. There were times that I did things in the school that the teachers didn't know about.
10. Occasionally I cover up my true feelings when I talk to my teachers.
11. I like all the teachers I've had in this school.
12. I am sure that this is the best school in the state.
13. The teachers I now have are as good as or better than teachers in a boarding or private school.
14. There is nothing that my teachers this term won't do to make a student happy and comfortable.
15. All students who are put on detention or made to remain after school deserve it since my teachers are always fair in their decisions.

16. I agree with everything my teachers want me to do.
17. There are times when I wish some of my teachers treated me better.
18. Sometimes my teachers don't want to be bothered by the students.
19. There are times when I feel that some of my teachers don't quite understand me.
20. Sometimes my teachers treat the more mature students as if they were children.
21. My teachers are not fit to teach us students.
23. Sometimes my teachers actually teach me something.
22. I have never had a single decent teacher in the school.
24. There are times when a student needs to be punished for breaking the rules of the school.
25. There are times when my teachers are right even though I may think they are wrong.
26. There is not a single good thing about being a student in this school.
27. I have not had one interesting teacher or activity in this school.
28. The teachers in this school always take advantage of the students.
29. At times I am interested in some subject and enjoy being in this school.
30. In some ways I get more attention in the school than I would outside.

RETARDATE ATTITUDE TEST

1. More money should be spent by people in the care and treatment of retardates.
2. Anyone who tries hard to better himself deserves the respect of others.
3. If this place had enough well-trained people working here, many of the retardates would improve enough to get out of the school.

4. It is better to be a person who is unimportant and honest than to be one who is important and dishonest.
5. A person would be foolish not to try to enjoy himself as long as he is in the state school.
6. In many ways living here is just like living in any other neighborhood you would find.
7. The superintendent (boss) of this school should try hard to get attendants who are able to get along with the retardates.
8. The best way to handle people is to tell them what they want to hear.
9. It is important not to think about the life you could lead outside this place as long as you live here.
10. More than anything else, the retardates need the respect and understanding of the people who work with them.
11. The best things this school can do for a retardate cannot help him unless he also tries to help himself.
12. The best way to fit into this place (get along) is to have a good time.
13. If you really want to, it is not too hard to leave this place.
14. It is possible to have a good life here.
15. Although retardates may seem all right when they have left here, they should not be allowed to marry.
16. The best way to handle retardates here is to keep them behind locked doors.
17. A person can be good in every way.
18. Regardless of how you look at it, retardates are no longer really human.
19. Once a retardate, always a retardate.
20. It's important for a retardate to have a sense of humor.
21. Never tell anyone the real reason you did something unless it will be helpful to you.
22. There is nothing wrong in being retarded.
23. There is little that can be done for retardates here except to see that they are comfortable and well-fed.
24. Anyone who completely trusts anyone else is asking for trouble.
25. All retardates in institutions should be prevented from having children by a painless operation.

26. An employer would be foolish to hire a retardate who had been here, even if he seems well-trained for the job.
27. There are many people on the outside more disturbed than retardates who have been here for a long time.
28. Most people won't work hard at things unless they are forced to.
29. It is helpful for retardates to spend most of their time relaxing and enjoying their stay here.
30. Being in this place is more helpful to a retardate than being at home or in a foster home.
31. It is a good thing to treat retardates with kindness but it will probably not help them to get any smarter.
32. It would be hard to develop a close friendship with a person who had been a retardate at this place.
33. People who were once retardates here are no more dangerous than anyone else.
34. People should be sure they are doing the right thing before they do it.
35. A retardate should try to make his life as simple as possible in this place.
36. Retardates should spend time getting to know more about themselves by sitting down alone and thinking.
37. If you want to, it is kind of easy to feel that you are not living at a state school.
38. Most retardates in this place are willing to work.
39. If I had grown up in a normal home, I wouldn't be here.
40. Retardates here should have something to say about how this place is run.
41. You have to get to know your matron if you want to get out of this place.
42. The best way to get help for your problems is to keep busy and forget you are a retardate.
43. Retardates here should have as much freedom as they want.
44. Even if a retardate who had been here seems better, he should not be given a driver's license.
45. It is important to learn all about this place if you want to get things done and enjoy yourself.
46. I don't think there should be places like this, but only places where you don't live in.

47. Sometimes an attendant or matron can be more important in making your stay here more comfortable than some of the big bosses in the institution.

48. Many retardates are capable of doing a good job (skilled labor) even though in some ways they are very disturbed.

49. The saying that there is a sucker (fool) born every minute is right.

50. When a person has a problem or a worry, it is best not to think about it, but keep busy with more pleasant things.

51. People who are retarded should never be treated in the same place with other kinds of people.

52. The only hope for a retardate here is to get understanding.

53. Anyone who is in an institution for the retarded should not be allowed to vote.

54. The law should allow a woman to divorce her husband as soon as he has been in a place like this.

55. A retardate should not think about leaving here but rather how he can get better.

56. The main purpose of a state school for the retarded should be to protect the public from retarded people.

57. Everyone should have someone in his life whose happiness means as much to him as his own.

58. Retardates should avoid jobs here because jobs make it easier for a person to want to stay here.

59. One of the best spots in this place is the canteen.

60. I know of retardates who are really well enough to leave, but they enjoy it here and want to stay.

61. A retardate should get to know the people who work here before he starts to get treated for his condition.

62. Most people who get ahead in the world lead good clean lives.

63. A retardate should never leave here until he is completely well.

64. A woman would be foolish to marry a retardate.

65. Every state school for the retarded should be surrounded by a high fence and guards.

66. The thing most retardates here need is a period of relaxation to get on their feet again.

67. A person who has been in a state school should not be allowed to be a mayor.
68. Most people are lonely.
69. If you want to get better, it's important to establish a comfortable routine here.
70. Retardates should have more say as to whether they should leave or stay here.
71. A place like this should not ask retardates to do things which they have not done on the outside.
72. As a retardate, one shouldn't spend time getting to know other retardates, especially those who live in other buildings.
73. If I get to live outside, I will try to hide that I was a retardate here.
74. The best way to learn about this place is to ask retardates who have been here for some time.
75. Most men are brave.
76. A retardate can't improve unless he is prepared to suffer a little.
77. Retardates here will feel better if this place did not bother them.
78. You should try to be on friendly terms with the attendants and matrons.
79. Everything a retardate does here, including goofing off (fooling around) helps him get better.
80. Retardates should be required to work at a job while they are here.
81. It would be good for retardates if this place told them what to do all the time.
82. Most retardates here are not as stupid as most people think.
83. Retardates would get better if matrons and attendants did not bother them so much.
84. Everybody has a little bit of something wrong with them.
85. You can be sure that most people have a mean streak and they will show it whenever they have a chance.
86. Retardates should be permitted to go into town whenever they want to.
87. It's a smart thing to be nice to important people.

88. A retardate should try to meet as many other retardates as possible, rather than just staying in his own building.
89. It is better not to make friends while you are here.
90. Honesty is always the best policy.
91. You should always do what the attendants and matrons tell you to do, even if you don't want to.
92. Most people are good and kind.
93. There are good reasons for lying sometimes.
94. Watching television is good for retardates.
95. Retardates always come to this place because they are forced to by others.
96. It is often better not to have visitors from home because they may upset you.
97. It is hard to get ahead without cheating.
98. Mental hospitals are better places than state schools.
99. It's kind of easy to fool the people who work here.
100. Most people who work here really don't know what we do at this place.

STAFF ATTITUDE TEST

1. More money should be spent by people in the care and treatment of retardates.
2. Anyone who tries hard to better himself deserves the respect of others.
3. If this place had enough well-trained people working here, many of the retardates would improve enough to get out of the school.
4. It is better to be a person who is unimportant and honest than to be one who is important and dishonest.
5. A person would be foolish not to try to enjoy himself as long as he is in the state school.
6. In many ways living here is just like living in any other neighborhood you would find.
7. The superintendent (boss) of this school should try hard

to get attendants who are able to get along with the retardates.

8. The best way to handle people is to tell them what they
want to hear.

9. It is important for a retardate not to think about the life
he could lead outside this place as long as he lives here.

10. More than anything else, the retardates need the respect
and understanding of people who work with them.

11. The best things this school can do for a retardate cannot
help him unless he also tries to help himself.

12. The best way for a retardate to fit into this place (get
along) is to have a good time.

13. If he really wants to, it is not too hard for a retardate to
leave this place.

14. It is possible for a retardate to have a good life here.

15. Although retardates may seem all right when they have
left here, they should not be allowed to marry.

16. The best way to handle retardates here is to keep them
behind locked doors.

17. A person can be good in every way.

18. Regardless of how you look at it, retardates are no longer
really human.

19. Once a retardate, always a retardate.

20. It's important for a retardate to have a sense of humor.

21. Never tell anyone the real reason you did something unless
it will be helpful to you.

22. There is nothing wrong in being retarded.

23. There is little that can be done for retardates here
except to see that they are comfortable and well-fed.

24. Anyone who completely trusts anyone else is asking for
trouble.

25. All retardates in institutions should be prevented from
having children by a painless operation.

26. An employer would be foolish to hire a retardate who had
been here, even if he seems well-trained for the job.

27. There are many people on the outside more disturbed than
retardates who have been here for a long time.

28. Most people won't work hard at things unless they are
forced to.

29. It is helpful for retardates to spend most of their time relaxing and enjoying their stay here.

30. Being in this place is more helpful to a retardate than being at home or in a foster home.

31. It is a good thing to treat retardates with kindness but it will probably not help them to get any smarter.

32. It would be hard to develop a close friendship with a person who had been a retardate at this place.

33. People who were once retardates here are no more dangerous than anyone else.

34. People should be sure they are doing the right thing before they do it.

35. A retardate should try to make his life as simple as possible in this place.

36. Retardates should spend time getting to know more about themselves by sitting down alone and thinking.

37. If he wants to, it is kind of easy for a retardate to feel that he is not living at a state school.

38. Most retardates in this place are willing to work.

39. If retardates had grown up in normal homes they wouldn't be here.

40. Retardates here should have something to say about how this place is run.

41. Retardates have to get to know their matrons if they want to get out of this place.

42. The best way for retardates to get help for their problems is to keep busy and forget they are retarded.

43. Retardates here should have as much freedom as they want.

44. Even if a retardate who had been here seems better, he should not be given a driver's license.

45. It is important for a retardate to learn all about this place if he wants to get things done and enjoy himself.

46. I don't think there should be places like this, but only places where retardates don't live in.

47. Sometimes an attendant or matron can be more important in making a retardate's stay here more comfortable than some of the big bosses in the institution.

48. Many retardates are capable of doing a good job (skilled labor) even though in some ways they are very disturbed.

49. The saying that there is a sucker (fool) born every minute is right.

50. When a person has a problem or a worry, it is best not to think about it, but keep busy with more pleasant things.

51. People who are retarded should never be treated in the same place with other kinds of people.

52. The only hope for a retardate here is to get understanding.

53. Anyone who is in an institution for the retarded should not be allowed to vote.

54. The law should allow a woman to divorce her husband as soon as he has been in a place like this.

55. A retardate should not think about leaving here but rather how he can get better.

56. The main purpose of a state school for the retarded should be to protect the public from retarded people.

57. Everyone should have someone in his life whose happiness means as much to him as his own.

58. Retardates should avoid jobs here because jobs make it easier for a person to want to stay here.

59. One of the best spots in this place is the canteen.

60. I know of retardates who are really well enough to leave but they enjoy it here and want to stay.

61. A retardate should get to know the people who work here before he starts to get treated for his condition.

62. Most people who get ahead in the world lead good clean lives.

63. A retardate should never leave here until he is completely well.

64. A woman would be foolish to marry a retardate.

65. Every state school for the retarded should be surrounded by a high fence and guards.

66. The thing most retardates here need is a period of relaxation to get on their feet again.

67. A person who has been in a state school should not be allowed to be a mayor.

68. Most people are lonely.

69. If a retardate wants to get better, it's important for him to establish a comfortable routine here.

70. Retardates should have more to say as to whether they should leave or stay here.
71. A place like this should not ask retardates to do things which they have not done on the outside.
72. As a retardate, one shouldn't spend time getting to know other retardates, especially those who live in other buildings.
73. If a retardate gets to live outside, he should try to hide that he was a retardate here.
74. The best way to find out about this place is to ask retardates who have been here for some time.
75. Most men are brave.
76. A retardate can't improve unless he is prepared to suffer a little.
77. Retardates here would feel better if this place did not bother them.
78. A retardate should try to be on friendly terms with the attendants and matrons.
79. Everything a retardate does here, including goofing off (fooling around), helps him get better.
80. Retardates should be required to work at a job while they are here.
81. It would be good for retardates if this place told them what to do all the time.
82. Most retardates here are not as stupid as most people think.
83. Retardates would get better if matrons and attendants did not bother them so much.
84. Everybody has a little bit of something wrong with them.
85. You can be sure that most people have a mean streak and they will show it whenever they have a chance.
86. Retardates should be permitted to go into town whenever they want to.
87. It's a smart thing to be nice to important people.
88. A retardate should try to meet as many other retardates as possible, rather than just staying in his own building.
89. It is better for a retardate not to make friends while he is here.
90. Honesty is always the best policy.

91. A retardate should always do what the attendants and matrons tell him to do, even if he doesn't want to.

92. Most people are good and kind.

93. There are good reasons for lying sometimes.

94. Watching television is good for retardates.

95. Retardates always come to this place because they are forced to by others.

96. It is often better that a retardate not have visitors from home because they may upset him.

97. It is hard to get ahead without cheating.

98. Mental hospitals are better places than state schools.

99. It's kind of easy for a retardate to fool the people who work here.

100. Most people who work here really don't know what retardates do at this place.

References

Ammons, R. B., and H. S. Ammons, *Full-Range Picture Vocabulary Test.* Missoula, Mont.: Psychological Test Specialists, 1948.

Ammons, R. B., and C. H. Ammons, *The Quick Test.* Missoula, Mont.: Psychological Test Specialists, 1962.

Arthur, G., Pseudo-feeblemindedness. *American Journal of Mental Deficiency,* 1947, *52,* 137–142.

Benda, C. E., Psychopathology of childhood. In L. Carmichael (ed.), *Manual of Child Psychology,* 2nd ed. New York: Wiley, 1954.

Benda, C. E., M. J. Farrell, and C. E. Chipman, The inadequacy of present day concepts of mental deficiency and mental illness in child psychiatry. *American Journal of Psychiatry,* 1951, *107,* 721–727.

Benda, C. E., N. D. Squires, M. J. Ogonik, and R. Wise, Personality factors in mild mental retardation: Part I. Family background and socio-cultural patterns. *American Journal of Mental Deficiency,* 1963, *68,* 24–40.

Benton, A. L., The concept of pseudo-feeblemindedness. *A.M.A. Archives of Neurological Psychiatry,* 1956, *75,* 379–388.

Bijou, S. W., A functional analysis of retarded development. In N. R. Ellis (ed.), *International Review of Research in Mental Retardation.* New York: Academic Press, 1966.

Binet, A., and T. Simon, *The Intelligence of the Feebleminded.* Baltimore: Williams & Wilkins, 1916.

Blabner, G., The myth of mental retardation. *The Training School Bulletin,* 1967, *63,* 149–152.

Braginsky, D., Machiavellianism and manipulative interpersonal behavior in children. *Journal of Experimental Social Psychology*, 1970, 6, 77–99.

Braginsky, D., Machiavellianism and manipulative interpersonal behavior in children: two exploratory studies. Doctoral dissertation. Number 67-3847, Ann Arbor: University Micro films, Inc., 1966.

Braginsky, B., D. Braginsky, and K. Ring, *Methods of Madness: The Mental Hospital as a Last Resort*. New York: Holt Rinehart and Winston, 1969.

Christie, R., Impersonal interpersonal orientations and behavior Unpublished research proposal, 1962.

Conant, J., *On Understanding Science*, New Haven: Yale University Press, 1947.

Delay, J., P. Pichot, and J. Perse, La notion de débilité mental camouflée. *Annals of Medical Psychology*, 1952, *110*, 615 619.

Dexter, L., On the politics of sociology of stupidity in our society *Social Problems*, Winter 1962, 9, 224.

Doll, E. A., The nature of mental deficiency. *Psychological Review*, 1940, 47, 395–415.

Ellis, N. R. (ed.), The stimulus trace in behavioral inadequac In *Handbook of Mental Deficiency*, New York: McGraw Hill, 1963.

Etzioni, A., *The Active Society: A Theory of Societal and Politic Processes*. New York: The Free Press, 1968.

Farber, B., *Mental Retardation: Its Social Context and Soc Consequences*. Boston: Houghton-Mifflin, 1968.

Fernald, N. E., The burden of feeblemindedness. *Journal of Ps choasthenics*, 1912, *17*, 87–111.

Ginzberg, E., and D. W. Bray, *The Uneducated*. New Yor Columbia University Press, 1953.

Goffman, E., *Presentation of Self in Everyday Life*. New Yor Doubleday, 1959.

ffman, E., *Asylums*. New York: Doubleday, 1961.

dstein, K., Concerning rigidity. *Character and Personality*, 1943, II, 209–226.

ber, R. F., A manual on terminology and classification in mental retardation. *American Journal of Mental Deficiency*, Monograph Supplement, 1959, *64*, No. 2.

ber, R. F., Mental retardation: concepts and classification. In Trapp, E., and P. Hunelstein (eds.), *Readings on the Exceptional Child*. New York: Appleton-Century-Crofts, 1962.

tt, M. L., and R. G. Gibby, *The Mentally Retarded Child*. Boston: Allyn and Bacon, 1958.

es, E. E., *Ingratiation*. New York: Appleton-Century-Crofts, 1964.

nner, L., Feeblemindedness: absolute, relative and apparent. *The Nervous Child*, 1948, *7*, 365–397.

nner, L., *A Miniature Textbook of Feeblemindedness*. New York: Child Care Publications, 1949.

nner, L., Emotional disturbances simulating mental retardation. *Public Health News*, 1957, *38*, 313–332.

k, S. A., and B. B. Weiner, The Onondega census: fact or artifact. *Exceptional Children*, 1959, *25*, 226–231.

unin, J., Experimental studies of rigidity: I. The measurement of rigidity in normal and feebleminded persons. *Character and Personality*, 1941(a), *9*, 251–273.

unin, J., Experimental studies of rigidity: II. The exploratory power of the concept of rigidity as applied to feeblemindedness. *Character and Personality*, 1941(b), *9*, 273–282.

unin, J., Intellectual development and rigidity. In R. G. Barker, J. S. Kounin, and J. F. Wright (eds.), *Child Behavior and Development*. New York: McGraw-Hill, 1943.

tter, F. E., The pseudo mental deficiency syndrome. *Journal of Mental Science*, 1959, *105*, 406–420.

hn, T., *The Structure of Scientific Revolutions*. Chicago: University of Chicago Press, 1962.

Lewin, K., *A Dynamic Theory of Personality*. New York: McGraw-Hill, 1936.

Luria, A. R., *Problems of Higher Nervous Activity in the Norma. and Nonnormal Child*. Moscow: Akad. Pedag. Nauk. RSFSR 1956.

Luria, A. R., *The Mentally Retarded Child*. London: Pergamo Press, 1963.

Maher, B. A., Intelligence and brain damage. In N. R. Ellis (ed.) *Handbook of Mental Deficiency*. New York: McGraw-Hil 1963.

Mancuso, J. C., and M. Dreisinger, A view of the historical an current development of the concept of intelligence. *Psycholog in the Schools*, 1969, 6, 137–151.

Merton, R. K., *Social Theory and Social Structure*, 2nd ed New York: The Free Press, 1967.

Miller, D., Worlds that fail. *Transaction*, Dec. 1967, 36–41.

Miller, S. M., F. Riessman, and A. A. Seagull, Poverty and sel indulgence: a critique of the non-deferred gratification pa tern. In L. A. Ferman, J. L. Kornbluh, and A. Haber (eds. *Poverty in America*. Ann Arbor: University of Michigan Pres 1968.

Morel, B. A., *Traité des Dégénérescences Physiques, Intellectuell et Morales de l'espèce Humaine*. Paris: Bailliere, 1857.

O'Connor, N., and B. Hermelin, Discrimination in reversal learnir in imbeciles. *Journal of Abnormal and Social Psychology*, 195 59, 409–413.

Osborn, W., Associative clustering in organic and familial retar ates. *American Journal of Mental Deficiency*, 1960, 65, 35 357.

Papageorgis, D., Pseudo-feeblemindedness and the concept mental retardation. *American Journal of Mental Deficienc 1963, 68, 340–344.

President's Panel on Mental Retardation, *A Proposed Program f National Action to Combat Mental Retardation*. Washingtc D. C.: GPO, 1962.

Redlich, F., and D. Freedman, *The Theory and Practice of Psychiatry*. New York: Basic Books, 1966.

Richman, B. F., H. N. Kellner, and D. Allen, Size constancy in retarded versus normal children: a developmental hypothesis. *Journal of Consulting and Clinical Psychology*, 1968, *32*, 579–582.

Robinson, H. B., and N. M. Robinson, *The Mentally Retarded Child: A Psychological Approach*. New York: McGraw-Hill, 1965.

Sarason, S. B., and J. Doris, *Pschological Problems in Mental Deficiency*. 4th ed. New York: Harper & Row, 1969.

Sarason, S. B., and T. Gladwin, Psychological and cultural problems in mental subnormality. In R. L. Masland, S. B. Sarason, and T. Gladwin, *Mental Subnormality*. New York: Basic Books, 1958.

Sarbin, T., Anxiety: the reification of a metaphor. *Archives of General Psychiatry*, 1964, *10*, 630–638.

Sarbin, T., On the futility of the proposition that some people be labeled mentally ill. *Journal of Consulting Psychology*, 1967, *31*, 447–453.

Scheff, T. J., *Being Mentally Ill: A Sociological Theory*. Chicago: Aldine, 1966.

Schooler, C., and D. Parkel, The overt behavior of chronic schizophrenics and its relationship to their internal state and personal history. *Psychiatry*, 1966, *29*, 67–77.

Siegel, P., and J. Foshee, Molar variability in the mentally defective. *Journal of Adnormal and Social Psychology*, 1960, *60*, 141–143.

Skinner, B. F., *Science and Human Behavior*. New York: Macmillan, 1953.

Spitz, H. H., Field theory in mental deficiency. In Ellis, N. (ed.), *Handbook of Mental Deficiency*. New York: McGraw-Hill, 1963.

Stearns, A., and A. Ullman, One thousand unsuccessful careers. *American Journal of Psychiatry*, 1949, *11*, 801–809.

Tannenbaum, F., *Crime and the Community*. New York: Columbia University Press, 1938.

Terman, L. M., *The Measurement of Intelligence: An Explanation of and a Complete Guide for the Use of the Stanford Revision and Extension of the Binet-Simon Intelligence Scale*. Boston: Houghton, 1916.

Turbayne, C., *Myth of Metaphor*. New Haven: Yale University Press, 1960.

U. S. Department of Health, Education, and Welfare. Mental Health Statistics: Current reports for MHB I–7. Bethesda, Md. Public Health Service, National Institute of Mental Health, April 1963.

Wunsch, W. L., The first complete tabulation of the Rhode Island Mental Deficiency Record. *American Journal of Mental Deficiency*, 1951, 55, 293–312.

Zigler, E., Mental retardation: current issues and approaches. In M. L., Hoffman, and L. W. Hoffman, (eds.), *Review of Child Development Research*, Vol. II. New York: Russell Sage Foundation, 1966(a).

Zigler, E., Research on personality structures in the retardate. In N. R. Ellis, (ed.), *International Review of Research in Mental Retardation*. New York: Academic Press, 1966(b).

Zigler, E., and S. Harter, Socialization of the mentally retarded. In D. C. Goslin, (ed.), *Handbook of Socialization Theory and Research*. New York: Rand McNally, 1969.

Index